Your Book of
Steam Railway
Preservation

The *Your Book* Series

Abbeys · Acting · Aeromodelling · Anglo-Saxon England · Aquaria · Archaeology · Astronomy · Ballet · Brasses · Breadmaking · Butterflies and Moths · Camping · Canals · The Way a Car Works · Card Games · Chess · Corn Dollies · Medieval and Tudor Costume · Dinghy Sailing · Embroidery · English Country Dancing · Film-Making · Fishes · Flower Arranging · Forestry · The Guitar · Gymnastics · Hovercraft · Industrial Archaeology · Judo · Landscape Drawing · Light · Magic · Men in Space · Mental Magic · Modelling · Music · Painting · Paper Folding · Parliament · Patchwork · Pet Keeping · Keeping Ponies · Prehistoric Animals · Prehistoric Britain · Pressed and Dried Flowers · Racing and Sports Cars · The Recorder · Sea Fishing · The Seashore · Secret Writing · Shell Collecting · Soccer · Steam Railway Preservation · Swimming · Survival Swimming and Life Saving · Table Tricks · Tall Ships · Tennis · Traction Engines · Watching Wild Life · Woodwork.

YOUR BOOK OF
STEAM RAILWAY PRESERVATION

P. J. G. RANSOM

faber and faber

*First published in 1982
by Faber and Faber Limited
3 Queen Square London WC1N 3AU
Printed in Great Britain by
Fakenham Press Limited, Fakenham, Norfolk
All rights reserved*

© *P. J. G. Ransom, 1982*

British Library Cataloguing in Publication Data

Ransom, P.J.G.
 Your book of steam railway preservation.
 1. Locomotives—Great Britain—History
 I. Title
 625.2'61   TJ603.4.G7
ISBN 01-571-11931-X

Contents

		page
Introduction		9
CHAPTER ONE	Railway History in Outline	11
CHAPTER TWO	The Development of Railway Preservation	27
CHAPTER THREE	Components of a Steam Railway, and how they work	38
CHAPTER FOUR	Operation and Maintenance	46
CHAPTER FIVE	Museums, Depots and Main Line Steam	58
CHAPTER SIX	The Principal Preserved Railways	71
Further Reading		87
Index		89

Introduction

To our Victorian ancestors, steam trains were the everyday means of travel. Then our grandparents and parents gradually found newer forms of transport more convenient, and turned to buses, cars, aeroplanes, electric trains and diesel trains instead. Steam locomotives were withdrawn and many railways closed.

Some people regretted the disappearance of steam trains and set about preserving what they could. The sights and sounds of steam locomotives, which might have disappeared altogether, are now again familiar in preservation.

There are in the British Isles about forty preserved operating steam railways, and about the same number of railway museums and steam depots. There are, too, innumerable books about particular railways, locomotives and other aspects of the subject; there are several general guides to railway preservation throughout the British Isles; but there are almost no straightforward introductions to the subject. Here is one.

Acknowledgements

I am particularly grateful to the following people who helped me during preparation of this book: the Reverend Eric Buck; Keith Catchpole; M. J. Draper; Norman Gurley; Moira Hunter; D. A. Idle; John Jeffery and colleagues on the Nene Valley Railway; Colin Mountford.

For illustrations

The Science Museum, London, 1, 34
The *Illustrated London News* Picture Library, 2, 3, 5
Crown Copyright, the National Railway Museum, York, 4, 6, 7, 10, 12, 21, 22, 35, 36, 37
Miss L. Hodgkin and the County Archivist of Durham, 9
David Eatwell, 14
Steve Le Cheminant, 15, 19, 26, 29, 31, 41, 50
Renold Ltd., 20
D. A. Idle, 25
Beamish North of England Open Air Museum, 39
David Wilcock, 43
Charles P. Friel, 44, 45
Norman Gurley, 47
A. Coutanche (aged 12 at date of photograph), 52
All other photographs are by the author.

Chapter One
RAILWAY HISTORY IN OUTLINE

There have been railways of one sort or another in Britain since about 1604, for some 378 years. For the first 163 years, their rails were of timber; on them ran waggons, and the waggon wheels had flanges to keep them on the rails. These "waggonways" were usually only a few miles long, were commonest around Newcastle upon Tyne, and often connected coal pits with harbours. Horses hauled the waggons, but wherever possible waggonways were laid out so that laden waggons could run gently down hill by gravity.

From 1767 onwards cast-iron rails came into use. Many short iron-railways or tramroads were built, either for private use, by mine-owners for instance, or for public use by canal companies. In 1801 Parliament passed an Act to incorporate the Surrey Iron Railway Company. When a railway company was incorporated, people could buy shares in it: each person contributed part of the money needed to build the line and became in effect a part-owner of it. This was the usual means by which railways were built. The Surrey Iron Railway was the first public railway independent of a canal and it was opened in 1803. It ran from the Thames at Wandsworth to Croydon. "Public railway" means a railway by which anyone could send goods, or, on later public railways which carried passengers, anyone could travel. Passenger traffic by rail started in 1807, on the Oystermouth Railway near Swansea; passengers were carried in horse-drawn coaches.

Steam pumps were first used in the early eighteenth century to pump water out of mines, and from them had evolved stationary steam engines. On some waggonways and early railways these were used with cables to haul waggons up steep gradients. Towards the end of the eighteenth century people were attempting to make steam-powered vehicles; the first steam railway locomotive that worked satisfactorily was designed by Richard Trevithick and built in 1804. Its basic principle was the same as that of all later steam locomotives, apart from experimental ones. Steam was generated in a boiler by the heat of a fire, and admitted alternately to each end of a cylinder. There, steam pressure drove a piston alternately backwards and forwards: the piston was connected by rods to a crank which revolved and turned the wheels.

Map of Museums, Railway Preservation Depots and Preserved Railways mentioned in *Your Book of Steam Railway Preservation*.

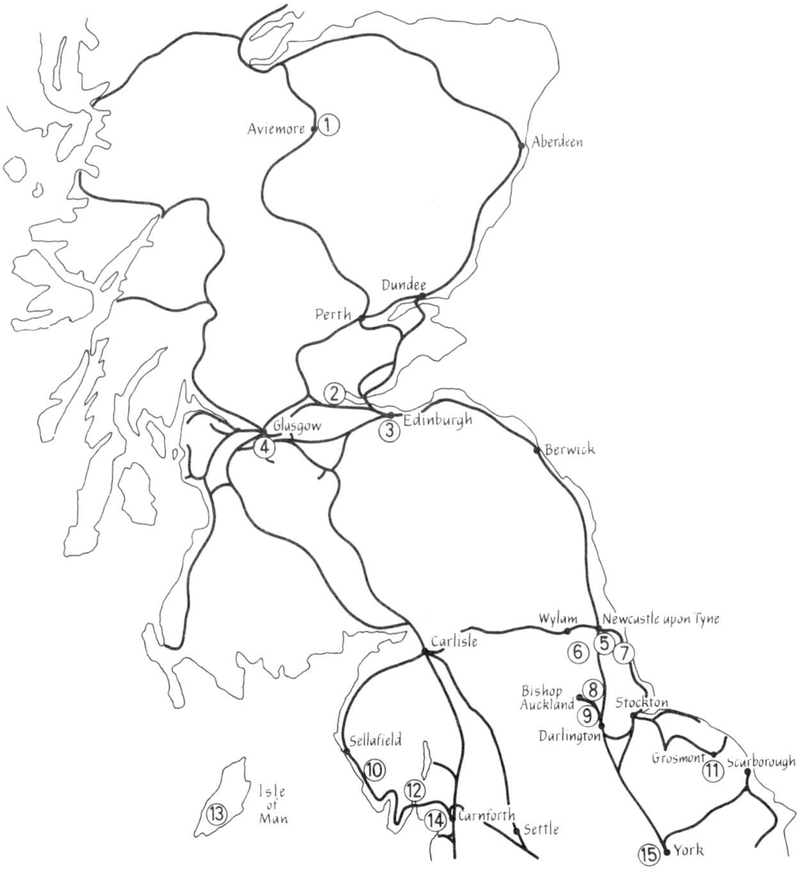

1. Strathspey Railway
2. Scottish Railway Preservation Society, Falkirk and Bo'ness
3. Royal Scottish Museum
4. Glasgow Museum of Transport
5. Bowes Railway
6. Beamish North of England Open Air Museum
7. Monkwearmouth Station Museum
8. Timothy Hackworth Museum, Shildon
9. North Road Station Museum
10. Ravenglass & Eskdale Railway
11. North Yorkshire Moors Railway
12. Lakeside & Haverthwaite Railway
13. Isle of Man Railways
14. Steamtown Railway Museum, Carnforth
15. National Railway Museum, York
16. Keighley & Worth Valley Railway
17. Middleton Railway
18. Steamport Transport Museum, Southport
19. North Western Museum of Science & Industry, Manchester
20. Dinting Railway Centre, Glossop
21. Merseyside County Museums, Liverpool
22. Llanberis Lake Railway
23. Snowdon Mountain Railway
24. Midland Railway Centre
25. Festiniog Railway
26. Foxfield Light Railway

27. North Norfolk Railway
28. Bala Lake Railway
29. Wolferton Station Museum
30. Great Central Railway
31. Chasewater Light Railway
32. Welshpool & Llanfair Light Railway
33. Talyllyn Railway
34. Nene Valley Railway
35. Severn Valley Railway
36. Birmingham Railway Museum, Tyseley
37. Bressingham Steam Museum
38. Bulmer Railway Centre, Hereford
39. Dowty Railway Preservation Society, Ashchurch
40. Gwili Railway
41. Leighton Buzzard Narrow Gauge Railway
42. Quainton Railway Centre
43. Brecon Mountain Railway
44. Norchard Steam Centre, Forest of Dean
45. Great Western Society, Didcot Railway Centre
46. Great Western Railway Museum, Swindon
47. Science Museum, South Kensington
48. London Transport Museum, Covent Garden
49. Welsh Industrial & Maritime Museum, Cardiff
50. Sittingbourne & Kemsley Light Railway
51. West Somerset Railway
52. Mid-Hants Railway
53. Kent & East Sussex Railway
54. Bluebell Railway
55. Romney, Hythe & Dymchurch Railway
56. Isle of Wight Steam Railway
57. Dart Valley Railway— Buckfastleigh line
58. Dart Valley Railway—Torbay line

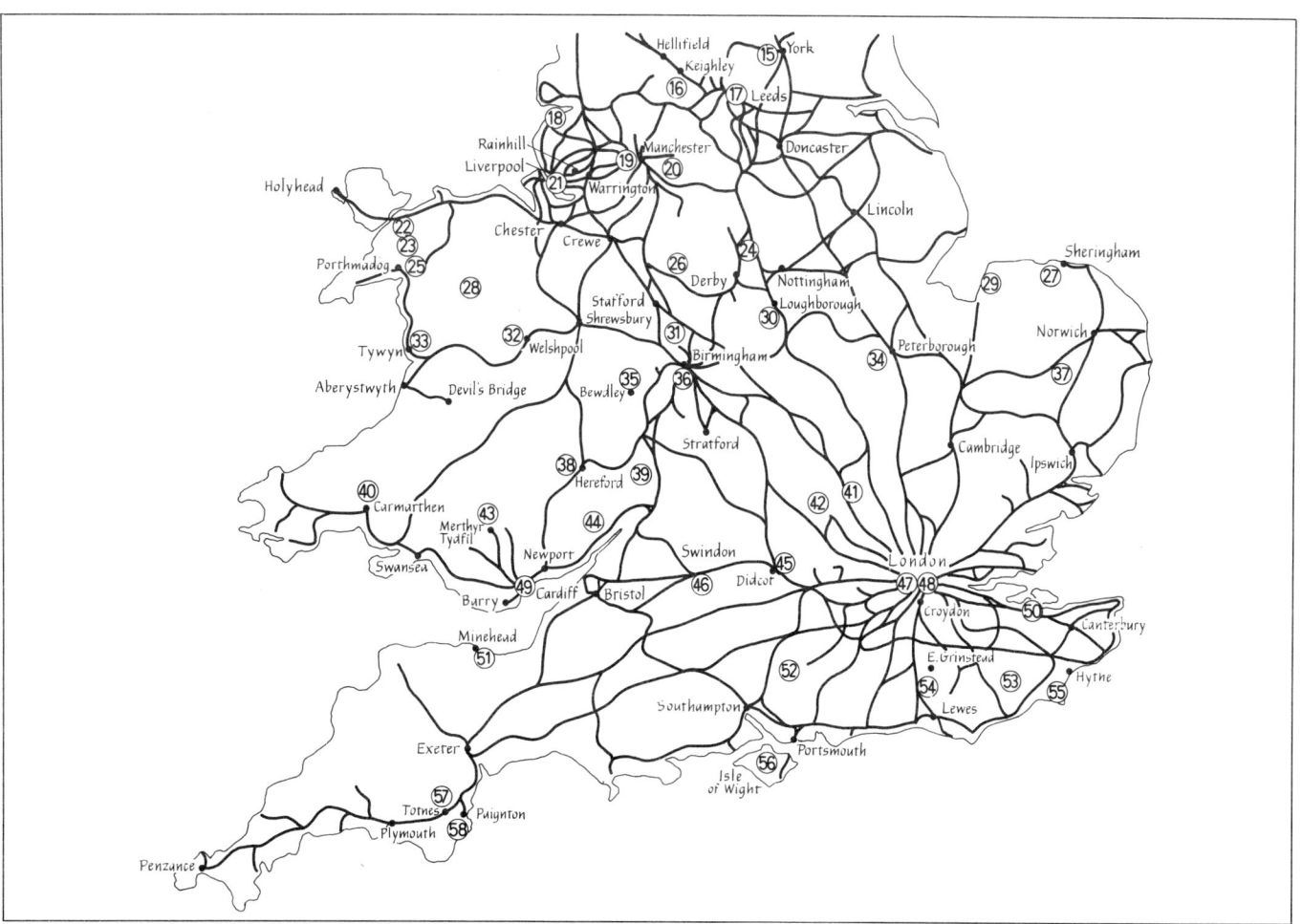

Trevithick's locomotive ran on the Penydarren Tramroad near Merthyr Tydfil in South Wales. Unfortunately it was too heavy and broke too many of the brittle cast-iron rails to be used regularly. About 1812, however, the price of horse fodder rose steeply and owners of colliery waggonways started to investigate the possibility of using coal-burning locomotives instead of horses. John Blenkinsop re-laid the Middleton Colliery waggonway, near Leeds, with iron rails and had a locomotive built by Matthew Murray. It started work in 1812 and, with others like it, ran satisfactorily for many years. It was propelled by a cog wheel which meshed with the teeth of a continuous rack beside one of the rails, because Blenkinsop and Murray thought that if they built a locomotive light enough for their track and driven by plain wheels, these would spin round instead of propelling it forwards.

Tests to establish that a locomotive of this kind would be heavy enough to be propelled by plain wheels were carried out by William Hedley, manager of Wylam Colliery near Newcastle upon Tyne. He then built several locomotives for the Wylam waggonway, which had been re-laid with iron rails a few years earlier. Two of his locomotives, *Puffing Billy* and *Wylam Dilly*, are preserved: the oldest existing locomotives. Their names originate from the workmen's custom of calling waggons "dillies". *Puffing Billy* was at first "the puffing dilly".

Among those who saw the Wylam locomotives at work was George Stephenson. Stephenson, then in his early thirties, was a self-educated genius: he had started work, as was then common, at the age of nine or ten and learned to read and write in his spare time at the age of eighteen. He completed his first locomotive, the *Blücher*, for the Killingworth Colliery railway, near Newcastle, in 1814.

Over the next few years Stephenson built improved locomotives and acquired the skills needed to lay out railways intended to be worked by them. In 1821 an Act of Parliament was passed for the Stockton & Darlington Railway, to link the port of Stockton with Darlington and coal mines near Bishop Auckland. Stephenson became the company's engineer: he was in charge of laying out and building the railway. In this work he was assisted by his son Robert Stephenson. The gauge, or width between the rails, which Stephenson used for this and other early steam railways was 4 ft. 8 in.; later, half an inch was added to produce the British standard gauge of 4 ft. 8½ in.

Much of the Stockton & Darlington Railway was laid with rails made of the newly-developed malleable iron. They were formed by passing the hot iron between rollers, so they were longer than cast-iron rails, gave a smoother ride, and were less brittle. They were suitable for locomotives—the S & DR was the first public railway built to be worked by locomotives as well as horses, and it was opened in 1825. The first train was hauled by the Stephensons' locomotive *Locomotion* and watched by immense crowds.

In 1826, Parliament passed an Act to incorporate the Liverpool & Manchester Railway. George Stephenson was appointed engineer. This was a new sort of railway: its purpose was to link two large cities as a trunk line for general traffic. But how this traffic was to be worked became a problem for its promoters, for the experience of the Stockton & Darlington Railway with locomotives was unhappy. Stephenson's early locomotives were satisfactory on short colliery tramroads, but over longer runs their boilers could not produce enough steam. The Stockton & Darlington considered abandoning the use of locomotives and relying instead on horses and the force of gravity to move the waggons.

The Liverpool & Manchester directors considered using stationary steam engines at intervals along the railway, to haul the trains along by cables. In 1827, however, Robert Stephenson returned, after three years in South America, and started to develop locomotive design rapidly; and in 1829 the L & MR directors decided to hold a competition for an improved locomotive. Three locomotives, *Rocket*, *Sans Pareil* and *Novelty*, took part in this competition, the Rainhill Trials. The winner, and the only one to do all that was asked of it, and more, was the famous *Rocket*. She proved conclusively that locomotives could power the Liverpool & Manchester Railway and similar lines.

1. The Liverpool & Manchester Railway at Edge Hill, Liverpool, about 1831. Cable haulage was used through the tunnels and locomotives were attached to trains at this point for the journey to Manchester.

Rocket had been built by Robert Stephenson for a partnership comprising himself, George Stephenson and Henry Booth. Booth was secretary of the L & MR company, and it was he who had earlier hit on the idea which would enable a boiler to make as much steam as possible. Hot gases and smoke from the fire were passed not, as hitherto, through a single large thick-walled flue surrounded by water, but instead through a great many small, thin-walled tubes. This arrangement enabled far more heat to be transferred to the water, to produce ample steam; it was the secret of *Rocket*'s success, and became the normal arrangement for locomotive boilers. Robert Stephenson continued to develop locomotive design. In 1830, for instance, cylinders steeply inclined to the rear, a conspicuous feature of *Rocket*, gave way on the locomotive *Planet* to horizontal cylinders, low down at the front of the locomotive. This too became the usual layout for subsequent locomotives.

RAILWAY HISTORY IN OUTLINE 17

2. By the 1850s, rail travel was common. Passengers and their luggage are going aboard a train of the Eastern Counties Railway.

The Liverpool & Manchester Railway was opened in 1830 and was a great success. Previously it had taken half a day to travel from Liverpool to Manchester by stage coach: the journey was reduced to a little over one hour by steam train. The advantages of building such trunk railways between other large cities were obvious; the first to be completed, in 1837, was the Grand Junction Railway, from Birmingham via Stafford to Warrington and Earlestown, where it joined the Liverpool & Manchester; the next was the London & Birmingham, between those two cities, in 1838. Other trunk lines completed soon afterwards included the London & Southampton, soon re-named the London & South Western, and the Great Western, between London and Bristol, engineered by Isambard Kingdom Brunel.

Most early trunk railways were successful, and more and more were promoted, particularly during the period known as the Railway Mania (1844–6). Not all were built, but out of that period did come many railways still important today. Other lines were built later; most important railways in Britain, and many branch lines, were built during the period 1835 to 1890. Amalgamations of railway companies, and take-overs of small ones by larger ones, continued throughout the Victorian and Edwardian period. For most of that time, however, and until 1922, railways in Britain were owned and operated by about twenty-five large railway companies and many other small ones; some railways were owned jointly by two or more companies.

RAILWAY HISTORY IN OUTLINE 19

3. (*opposite*) The Royal Albert Bridge over the Tamar, at Saltash, near Plymouth, was designed by Brunel and completed in 1859.

4. The Victorian railway at its greatest: an LNWR express approaches Shap summit hauled by a "Jumbo" class locomotive. Preserved locomotive *Hardwicke* (see page 61) is of this class.

The principal railways, then, were the following, in descending order of size:
Great Western Railway (GWR) with main lines from London (Paddington) to Exeter, Plymouth and Penzance, to Bristol and South Wales, and to Birmingham and the West Midlands;
Midland Railway (MR) centred on Derby, with main lines radiating to London (St Pancras), to Birmingham and Bristol, to Manchester, to Leeds and Carlisle, and to Nottingham and Lincoln;
London & North Western Railway (LNWR) with main lines from London (Euston) to Birmingham, Crewe, Liverpool, Manchester, Carlisle, and Holyhead for ships to Ireland. The Liverpool & Manchester, Grand Junction, and London & Birmingham companies were all merged into the LNWR;

5. Everyone travelled by train in Victorian times. These children are setting off for a country holiday in 1889.

North Eastern Railway (NER) with main line from a junction with the Great Northern Railway (see below) near Doncaster to York, Newcastle and Berwick. The Stockton & Darlington was merged into the NER;
North British Railway (NBR) with main lines radiating from Edinburgh to Berwick, Carlisle, Glasgow and Dundee;
Great Eastern Railway (GER) with main lines from London (Liverpool Street) via Ipswich and via Cambridge to Norwich;
Caledonian Railway (CR) with main lines from Carlisle to Edinburgh, Glasgow, Perth and Aberdeen;
Great Northern Railway (GNR) with main line from London (King's Cross) to Doncaster and Leeds;
London & South Western Railway (LSWR) with main lines from London (Waterloo) to Portsmouth, Southampton, Exeter and Plymouth.

6. High speed steam train: the LNER put on the *Silver Jubilee* express in 1935.

Other important companies included the Highland Railway (HR), the Great North of Scotland Railway (GNSR), the Glasgow & South Western Railway (GSWR), the Furness Railway (FR), the Lancashire & Yorkshire Railway (L&YR), the North Staffordshire Railway (NSR), the Great Central Railway (GCR), the Cambrian Railways (CR), the London, Brighton & South Coast Railway (LB&SCR), and the South Eastern & Chatham Railway (SE&CR).

Most large companies operated not only their main and branch lines but also suburban lines around large cities. Railways of specialized types were developed, too. Underground railways provided transport in large and crowded cities—steam-operated at first, they were among the first to be electrified, from the 1890s onwards. Railways of narrow gauge—in some instances as narrow as 1 ft. 11½ in.—were built in hilly districts, particularly North Wales. They could traverse sharp curves, so construction costs were low because cuttings, embankments and so on were smaller than those needed for standard gauge lines. In 1896 the Light Railways Act enabled railways (of standard or narrow gauge) to be built cheaply in rural areas which otherwise could not afford them: these light railways were authorized by light railway order, a Government decree cheaper to obtain than an Act of Parliament. Light railways could also be operated more cheaply than ordinary railways. Main line safety standards were relaxed—for instance, signals were few, and many level crossings had no gates—but in return for this trains had to go slowly. Light railway orders could also authorize existing railways to be worked cheaply as light railways, and this provision later became important when preserved railways were being set up, as mentioned on page 32.

Throughout the railway era, privately owned mineral and industrial railways, of both standard and narrow gauges, were also much used. Many of them were connected to the main railway system.

From about 1850 until the First World War railways had almost a monopoly of inland transport. To travel anywhere for more than a short distance was almost certain to mean going by train, and most goods went by train too. To keep fares and rates down, the Government encouraged railway companies to compete against one another for traffic. In consequence there were in many instances two or even three routes, between the same places, belonging to different companies. The list of companies given above includes some examples. Throughout this period improvements were made in the designs of locomotives and coaches. Trains grew heavier and larger locomotives were built to haul them. Rails of steel, more hard-wearing than iron, were introduced in the 1860s.

During the First World War, 1914–18, railways were much used, but at the same time they lost many of their staff to the armed forces. They were badly maintained, and by the end of the war were in poor condition. During the war railways had been under Government control and this experience suggested that grouping railways together into larger units than the existing companies would have advantages. In 1923, therefore, at "the Grouping", most railway companies were amalgamated into four large ones.

Of the old main line companies, the Great Western alone kept its identity. It absorbed the Cambrian Railways and several smaller companies. Largest of the "big four" was the London, Midland & Scottish Railway (LMS): it incorporated the LNW, Midland, L&Y, Furness, Caledonian, GSW and Highland Railways. The London & North Eastern (LNER) included the Great Eastern, Great Northern, Great Central, North Eastern, North British and Great North of

7. More typical of the 1930s than the *Silver Jubilee* was this cross-country local train approaching Midford, Somerset & Dorset Joint Railway.

Scotland Railways; the Southern (SR) was composed of the LSWR, LB & SCR, and SE & CR. Many lesser companies also were absorbed by the new big companies.

At this period the railway network was still expanding: it reached a peak of 20,443 miles of route in 1927. But it was also meeting increasing competition from motor transport on the roads, which had been developing since the turn of the century. Motor cars and buses were often more convenient for passengers than trains; motor lorries carried goods from door to door without trans-shipment at stations. From 1927 onwards the railway network started to contract. Although new lines were built and opened—as they still are—their total length was less than that of existing branch lines which were closed because they could not meet road competition.

The railways did, however, speed up their main line trains to compete with road transport. This trend led to the streamlined expresses of the LMS and the LNER in the late 1930s, and culminated with the world record speed, for a steam locomotive, of 126 mph reached by the LNER locomotive *Mallard* in 1938. It remains unbeaten. The railways were also starting to use diesel power. The diesel engine has greater thermal efficiency than the steam engine: that is to say, more of the heat, produced by burning fuel, is converted into work. A diesel locomotive is instantly available, at the press of a button, instead of taking several hours to raise steam; and it needs only a driver, instead of a driver and fireman. The LMS started to replace steam-shunting locomotives by diesels, and the GWR started to introduce diesel railcars. The Southern electrified many of its routes, for passenger trains. Advantages of electric power over steam included better acceleration (leading to quicker journeys) and cleanliness. But diesel locomotives were expensive, and electrifying a railway more so, and the railway companies continued to depend mainly on steam.

During the Second World War (1939–45) railways were again over-used and under-maintained. In 1948 public transport in Britain was nationalized, and the railways of the big four companies, and most surviving small ones, were transferred to the newly formed British Transport Commission. This operated them under the name British Railways and divided the national railway network up into six regions: London Midland, Western, Southern, Eastern, North Eastern and Scottish. The North Eastern Region was eventually merged with the Eastern. In 1962 the BTC was disbanded and the British Railways Board established to own and run the railways. This it still does; it started to use the short title British Rail in 1965.

Back in the early 1950s, the railways of Britain, overworked in wartime and under-used in peacetime, were run-down and extremely old fashioned. While on the Continent and in North America railways were rapidly adopting electric or diesel traction, British Railways introduced a range of standard steam locomotives. In 1954, however, it at last started to use diesel multiple unit trains (DMUs), and in 1955 the BTC produced a comprehensive plan to modernize its railways. This envisaged, among much else, electrifying some main lines and replacement of steam by diesel traction in some other areas. At that

8. The last steam locomotive built for British Railways was *Evening Star*, completed in 1960. Now preserved, she is seen here taking part in the Rainhill cavalcade in 1980.

date, BR still had 19,000 steam locomotives.

The next fifteen years brought immense changes to the railway system. Before the modernization plan had had time to take effect, the railways, which had previously managed to pay their way, started to lose more and more money each year. This was a time of rapidly increasing prosperity, when many people bought cars for the first time and ceased to use public transport regularly. Dr Richard Beeching—now Lord Beeching—was appointed chairman of the BTC in 1961 and became chairman of the British Railways Board when it was established. After making detailed studies of railway traffic he produced his report, *The Re-shaping of British Railways* (often called "the Beeching Plan") in 1963.

The basic problem was that most of the railway system was still laid out as it had been when people were dependent on slow horse-drawn transport to reach the nearest station. This meant that branch lines, and wayside stations on main lines, were still common, but were little used now that people found it more convenient to go by car or bus to large stations served by fast trains, or indeed to make their entire journeys by road. Things were much the same with freight traffic. The report proposed closure of 2,363 passenger stations and halts out of a total of 4,709, and withdrawal of passenger trains from 5,000 miles of route out of a total of about 17,000. Most (but not all) of these closures were carried out between 1963 and 1970. Closures on such a large scale provoked great bitterness: the newspapers called the process the Beeching Axe.

During the same period diesel and electric trains and locomotives were replacing steam locomotives much more quickly than was originally intended. British Rail withdrew its last steam locomotives (apart from the three narrow gauge locomotives still used on its Vale of Rheidol tourist line) in 1968.

Since Lord Beeching's name is generally associated with closures and similar negative activities, it is important to realize that the present-day railway system is largely based on his positive proposals. The essence of his report was not only that railways should cease to be used for those things they do badly, but also that they *should* be used for those things they do well. This meant improvement of inter-city passenger train services—hence the Inter-City network; improvement of bulk freight trains—hence the many trains which now carry coal, oil and other materials in bulk, by the train-load; and introduction of scheduled "liner trains" to carry freight containers over the long-distance parts of their journeys which start and finish by road—hence the Freightliner system. From the user's point of view the present-day railway system, though less extensive than that of twenty-five years ago, is in many respects a vast improvement on it. To give but one example, in 1954 the *Flying Scotsman* express was scheduled to take 7 hours 37 minutes to travel from London to Edinburgh: now it takes 4 hours 35 minutes. This sort of improvement is not uncommon.

Such is human nature, though, that the modernization of the railways also gave an immense boost to enthusiasm for preserving what was best and most appealing of the steam railway age. This is described in the next chapter.

Chapter Two
THE DEVELOPMENT OF RAILWAY PRESERVATION

Probably the first historic locomotive to be preserved was *Invicta*. This locomotive was built by Robert Stephenson for the opening of the Canterbury & Whitstable Railway in 1830, and, though not very successful, was still present when the line was taken over by the South Eastern Railway in the late 1840s. Instead of scrapping her the SER preserved the locomotive in its works at Ashford, Kent. It was not until 1906, however, that she was placed on public display in Canterbury, and in Canterbury, after restoration for her 150th anniversary in 1980, she is still.

9. The first locomotive to be preserved and displayed in public, in 1857, was Stockton & Darlington Railway no. 1 *Locomotion*.

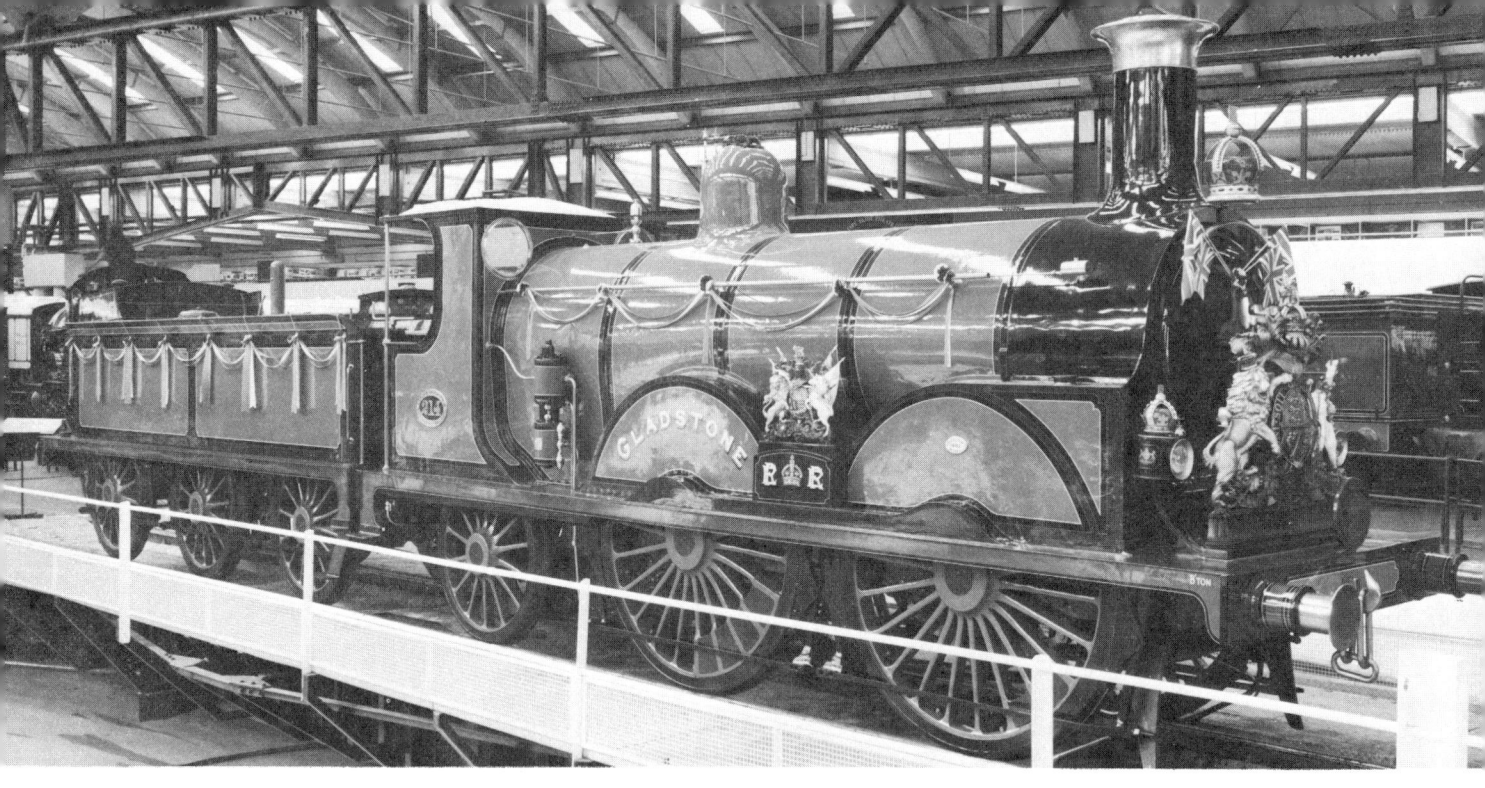

10. *Gladstone* of the LB & SCR became in 1927 the first locomotive saved for preservation by a voluntary society, the Stephenson Locomotive Society. She is seen here in the National Railway Museum, decorated as though to haul a royal train.

The first locomotive to be deliberately preserved and placed on public display was the Stockton & Darlington Railway's *Locomotion*, which had been driven by George Stephenson at the opening of the railway in 1825. In 1857 the S&DR placed her on a pedestal outside its main station, Darlington North Road. Today most of the station itself has become a museum and *Locomotion* is displayed within it.

Other locomotives were preserved in the early 1860s. The Stephensons' *Rocket*, or what was left of her, reached the Patent Office Museum, South Kensington, in 1862, and *Sans Pareil*, one of her competitors at the Rainhill Trials, rejoined her

THE DEVELOPMENT OF RAILWAY PRESERVATION 29

11. *Lion* was built for the Liverpool & Manchester Railway in 1837, and is now the oldest steamable locomotive in Britain.

there in 1864. Already, in 1862, the even older Wylam locomotive *Puffing Billy* (built in 1814) had reached South Kensington; sister locomotive *Wylam Dilly* eventually went, twenty years later, to the Royal Scottish Museum, Edinburgh, where she is still displayed.

After this burst of activity, things quietened down, although very occasionally a railway company would preserve a favoured locomotive on withdrawal, rather than scrap it, and in 1922 the North Eastern Railway established a museum at York to house such relics. In 1927 *Gladstone*, a popular and well-known locomotive, was, on withdrawal by the Southern Railway, purchased by the Stephenson Locomotive Society; this was the first occasion when a group of railway enthusiasts purchased a locomotive for preservation. *Gladstone* was displayed, but not in working order, in the York railway museum.

At the same period the approach of the centenary year (1930) of the Liverpool & Manchester Railway had aroused interest in the L & MR locomotive *Lion*, which had been built in 1837 and, remarkably, survived in use, powering a stationary pump in Liverpool docks. The docks board replaced her by new pumping machinery and presented her to the Liverpool Engineering Society; the locomotive was then restored to full working order by the LMS to take part in the L & MR centenary

12. The first railway enthusiasts' special with a historic locomotive ran in 1938 and is seen here at Peterborough hauled by preserved Great Northern Railway no. 1.

celebrations. She was overhauled again for the 150th anniversary celebrations in 1980 and is now the oldest workable locomotive in Britain. This locomotive now belongs to Merseyside County Museums, Liverpool.

In 1938 the LNER wished to publicize the introduction of new coaches and a streamlined locomotive for the old-established *Flying Scotsman* express. So it restored to working order Great Northern Railway express locomotive no. 1, which had been built in 1870 and preserved since withdrawal in 1907; this hauled some coaches of the same period to represent the *Flying Scotsman* train of sixty or seventy years before, and the old and the new trains were photographed alongside one another. Then, soon afterwards, no. 1 and train were chartered for an excursion by the Railway Correspondence & Travel Society: this was the first time an enthusiasts' society organized a special train hauled by a historic, preserved locomotive.

The era of railway preservation—complete railways, that is, rather than locomotives and other equipment—commenced in 1950 with the formation of the Talyllyn Railway Preservation Society. The 2 ft. 3 in. gauge Talyllyn Railway then had two locomotives, four coaches and a brake van all dating from the 1860s, some goods wagons, and a seven-mile route

THE DEVELOPMENT OF RAILWAY PRESERVATION 31

among the Welsh mountains. All of it was in very bad condition. Too unimportant to be nationalized, the TR had been kept going by the benevolence of its elderly sole shareholder, Sir Haydn Jones. He died in 1950.

13. In December 1955 a working party of volunteers is helping to maintain the Talyllyn, the first railway preserved entire.

The TRPS, the first railway preservation society, was formed by L. T. C. Rolt and friends to raise funds and voluntary labour to repair, maintain and run the railway with its locomotives and rolling stock. Sir Haydn's widow generously made an agreement with the society which, in effect, gave it control of the railway. The preserved Talyllyn ran its first trains in May 1951 and has since gone on from strength to strength, becoming much busier, with tourist passengers, than it ever was before.

That it would be able to do so was far from obvious at first, because of the enormous amount of work needed to bring the railway into good condition. When a few years later the Festiniog Railway Society was formed to revive the Festiniog Railway, Talyllyn supporters resented it: they thought there would not be sufficient support for two similar ventures, so that both would fail. This attitude was understandable at the time, however quaint it seems now. The 1 ft. 11½ in. gauge Festiniog Railway, which dated from 1832 and had pioneered narrow gauge steam locomotives in the 1860s, had been closed in 1946 and was derelict. In 1954 Alan Pegler purchased sufficient shares to control the railway company (later he gave them to a charitable trust) and the railway has been re-opened gradually, with voluntary labour and support from the society.

14. (*opposite*) In the 1950s British Railways were introducing standard steam locomotives, many of which are themselves now preserved. No. 70000 *Britannia* is on the Nene Valley Railway.

The first two standard gauge, full size, railways to be preserved re-opened almost simultaneously in 1960: the Middleton Railway and the Bluebell Railway. The Middleton Railway, on the southern outskirts of Leeds, originated as early as 1758 as the colliery waggonway which Blenkinsop and Murray were later to operate with their early steam locomotives. Subsequently it had become an ordinary colliery railway, and when part of this went out of use in 1959, the Middleton RPS (later the Middleton Railway Trust) was formed to preserve it. Unusually, for many years it concentrated mainly on freight traffic, to link factories along its route with British Rail. Passengers are carried at weekends, in brake vans and open wagons.

The Bluebell Railway, from Sheffield Park to Horsted Keynes in Sussex, is a five-mile section of the cross-country line which formerly ran from East Grinstead to Lewes, and which travellers affectionately called "the bluebell line" from the bluebell woods along its route. The line was closed in 1958. It became the first closed section of British Railways to be re-opened by a preservation society: to achieve this, the Bluebell Railway Preservation Society formed a company, Bluebell Railway Ltd; British Railways (after long negotiations) agreed to lease the line to the new company, and obtained light railway orders to make the line a light railway and authorize its transfer. Later on, Bluebell Railway Ltd bought the line from BR.

Since 1960 many other closed BR lines have been re-opened independently as preserved railways by means of light railway orders. There are details of the most important of these, and of other preserved railways, in Chapter 6. Most of them perpetuate the steam train era by using steam locomotives to haul passenger trains which visitors ride in. Most, too, are operated by a mixture of volunteers, who work on the railway in their spare time, and paid staff. The volunteers are usually members of the appropriate preservation society or similar group.

In some cases the preservation society controls the railway. In others, it acts as a supporters' club, and control of the railway rests with its shareholders, who are

THE DEVELOPMENT OF RAILWAY PRESERVATION 33

34 THE DEVELOPMENT OF RAILWAY PRESERVATION

15. Steam railway preservation covers more than just locomotives. Oakworth station on the Worth Valley Railway is maintained in Victorian style and has been seen in many films and television programmes, from *The Railway Children* onwards.

often those people who have put up the money to buy the line from BR. Generally there are close links between society and company—volunteers may also be shareholders, for instance. There are, however, many differences of detail in the ways in which different preserved railways are administered; but all are run for their own sake—I do not know of any line using volunteers which regularly pays a dividend to shareholders.

At the time when modernization plans were resulting in withdrawal of BR steam locomotives and much of the rolling stock which went with them, British Railways, despite financial problems, set aside a representative selection of steam locomotives and coaches for preservation. This today forms the nucleus of the national collection. It belongs now to the Department of Education and Science, and its principal home is the National Railway Museum, York. This was opened in 1975 and replaced both the earlier York railway museum and the BTC's former museum at Clapham, London.

Besides this, from the late 1950s onwards many steam locomotives were purchased, on withdrawal, for preservation. Some were bought by individuals and others by groups or societies many of which were set up for this purpose. At first many of these locomotives were small, narrow gauge industrial locomotives. In 1962 no. 9017, a passenger locomotive of the former Great Western Railway, was purchased from BR by a fund set up by T. R. Gomm; she was taken to the Bluebell Railway and set to work there, the first instance of an arrangement which has since become common. Many of the locomotives and coaches on preserved railways belong not to the operating company but to other preservation societies or to individuals.

Elsewhere, preservation depots were set up to house and maintain preserved locomotives and rolling stock. There is more about these in Chapter 5. Rapid increase in the number of preservation groups led to establishment of the Association of Railway Preservation Societies, to encourage them to co-operate and to run themselves soundly, and to publicize them. In 1965 nine societies were members of the association; now there are about eighty, with as many more as associates.

Some purchasers of steam locomotives were able to arrange for them to run on BR hauling special trains, notably Alan Pegler with his purchase of the famous LNER locomotive *Flying Scotsman* in 1963. But the end of steam on BR in 1968 was accompanied by withdrawal of all facilities for servicing steam locomotives, and BR imposed a general ban on the operation of privately owned steam locomotives over its tracks. Where steam trains had recently been familiar, they had disappeared, quite suddenly, for ever. Or so it seemed, until at last in 1972 BR relented and started to allow steam specials again. Now they are powered by locomotives maintained in preservation depots and run mostly over secondary main lines where they are unlikely to impede inter-city expresses. And although on preserved railways operated under light railway orders train speeds are strictly limited, on BR steam specials reach speeds of 60 mph or more. Because coaches suitable for use with steam locomotives are now going out of service on BR, SLOA, the Steam Locomotive Operators' Association, has acquired a set of Pullman Cars which are used in steam excursion trains.

The end of steam on BR meant also that the source of locomotives for preservation dried up—but public enthusiasm was still

16. GWR no. 3217 is ready to leave Sheffield Park, Bluebell Railway. This locomotive, at one time numbered 9017, was the first set to work on a preserved railway after purchase by an independent fund.

17. The 1975-built replica of S&DR *Locomotion* is often seen working at Beamish attached to chaldron waggons of the type traditional in North East England.

growing. The continuing demand for locomotives has been met in three main ways.

The first of these has been purchase of locomotives from private industrial railways serving mines and factories. These continued to be available and although they are generally not of types intended for hauling passenger trains, some have been successfully used for this purpose.

The second way has been import of locomotives from abroad; some of these were originally built in Britain for export. Standard gauge locomotives obtained from Continental countries are unable to run over British Rail because they are built to larger loading gauges—that is, they are too high and too wide. They can run, however, on certain preserved lines where clearances are large enough.

The third main recent source of locomotives for preservation has been repurchase of locomotives sold by BR for scrap, particularly from Woodham Bros. of Barry, South Wales. Unlike most scrap merchants, Woodham Bros. did not immediately cut up the locomotives they bought. Although these had been sold by BR on condition that they were not resold, the ARPS and the Midland 4F Preservation Society were able in 1968 to negotiate the release of the first, a class 4F locomotive built by the Midland Railway. Subsequently over 140 locomotives have been sold by Woodhams for preservation and, at the time of writing, sales continue. But the task of restoring the remaining Barry locomotives gets steadily more daunting. The best have long since gone, and the remainder have been parked in the open air for fourteen years or more. In the long run, however, it does seem likely that anything left at Barry which is worth preserving will be preserved.

The greatest gatherings of preserved locomotives have been those at Shildon, Co. Durham, in 1975 to celebrate the 150th anniversary of the opening of the Stockton & Darlington Railway, and in 1980 at Rainhill, near Liverpool, to celebrate the 150th anniversary of the Liverpool & Manchester Railway. For the 1975 event, a working replica of Stephenson's original S&DR locomotive *Locomotion* was built, and for the 1980 event working replicas of the Rainhill Trials locomotives *Rocket*, *Sans Pareil* and *Novelty* were constructed. On each occasion, replica and preserved locomotives paraded past spectators along a part of the original route of the line concerned.

Chapter Three
COMPONENTS OF A STEAM RAILWAY, AND HOW THEY WORK

Track—good track—is the first essential of any railway. Without it, no trains can run. It provides a smooth path for them, guides them, spreads their weight over the ground beneath. Its two steel rails are supported on cross-sleepers which also keep them to correct gauge; the sleepers, usually of wood but sometimes of concrete or steel, rest in a bed of ballast—small stones, often granite chippings—which keep them from moving when a train passes over the track.

Traditionally, most British Railways were laid with "bullhead" rail: in cross-section a thin centre has bulbous projections top and bottom to give strength without excessive weight (and cost). The French more graphically call this type of rail *double-champignon*, double mushroom. The upper projection is larger than the lower, to provide the running surface.

18. Bullhead rail (foreground) adjoins flat bottom rail on the Nene Valley Railway. The photograph shows the various parts.

KEY
1 Flat Bottom Rail
2 Base Plate
3 Fishplate
4 Ballast
5 Sleeper
6 Chair
7 Key
8 Bullhead Rail

COMPONENTS OF A STEAM RAILWAY, AND HOW THEY WORK 39

Bullhead rails are carried in cast-iron supports called "chairs", and held there by oblong "keys" of wood or spring steel; the chairs themselves are bolted or screwed to the sleepers.

An alternative type of rail is "flat bottom": in cross-section, the lower bulbous projection is replaced by a horizontal cross-piece, like a T upside down. Spikes are the simplest means of fastening such rails to sleepers; more substantial forms of flat bottom track incorporate screws, clips and/or baseplates of various types.

Rail ends are traditionally joined together by fishplates, which are rectangular steel plates positioned one each side of the rails at the joint and secured by bolts which pass through both fishplates and rail ends. On modernized railways most joints are welded and the familiar clickety-click train noise is absent. Points enable a train to diverge from one track to another—the name "points" derives from the pair of rails with chamfered ends which are moved to one side or the other to direct trains in the direction required.

19. Victoria Bridge, completed in 1861 and now one of the largest bridges on a preserved railway, carries the Severn Valley Railway across the River Severn.

40 COMPONENTS OF A STEAM RAILWAY, AND HOW THEY WORK

20. (*opposite*) This sectioned Isle of Man Railway locomotive now belongs to the North Western Museum of Science and Industry, Manchester, and enables the internal parts of a locomotive to be seen.

KEY
1 Fire Box
2 Boiler Barrel
3 Boiler Tubes
4 Steam Dome
5 Regulator Valve
6 Smoke Box
7 Piston
8 Cylinder
9 Driving Wheel
10 Coupling Rod

More complex forms of pointwork and crossings are used where space is too limited for successive turnouts. Illustration no. 43 gives the idea.

The adhesion between smooth steel wheels and smooth steel rails is much less than that between, say, rubber tyres and a tarmac road. So railways cannot normally have steep gradients. A gradient of 1 in 30 on a railway is steep, and most lines are much more easily graded. To make trackbeds level enough, when railways were (or are) built, cuttings and tunnels are needed through high ground, and embankments and viaducts across valleys. Over- and under-bridges carry roads above and beneath railways, and larger bridges and viaducts carry them over rivers and estuaries which lie in their path.

Although track is essential and civil engineering works such as viaducts are in some places spectacular, the chief attraction of preserved steam railways is nevertheless the locomotives. Something of the workings of a steam locomotive can be gathered from the illustration on page 40, which shows a sectioned locomotive: parts have been cut away to reveal other parts usually hidden. The firebox can be seen towards the rear: the fire burns fiercely within the inner firebox. On top and on each side this is jacketed by water to which some of the heat is transmitted. The cylindrical boiler barrel and boiler tubes can be seen clearly; hot gases from the fire pass through the tubes, transmitting more heat to the boiler water on their way to the smokebox at the front, from which they are ejected up the chimney. The steam dome is on top of the boiler, about half-way along. Within it is the regulator valve: a rod from the cab enables the driver to open and close this to regulate whether and how much steam passes from boiler to cylinders, and so to start and stop the locomotive and make it go faster or slower. Slide valves adjacent to the cylinders are operated automatically by rods and levers from the driving axle (not visible in the picture); they admit steam alternately to each end of the cylinders and simultaneously allow steam from the opposite ends to pass to the exhaust. So used steam is exhausted up the chimney at the end of the each piston stroke, to draw the fire.

To keep driving wheels from slipping, so far as possible, they are coupled together by rods. This locomotive has four driving wheels, and a further pair of wheels at the front, used only to carry part of the locomotive's weight and, since they swivel, to lead her into curves. Her wheel arrangement, therefore, is described as 2–4–0. The wheel arrangement of a locomotive is often mentioned to indicate its size and type; wheel arrangements range from 0–4–0 (four driving wheels only) for the smallest locomotives to 4–6–2 (four leading wheels followed by six driving wheels followed in turn by two trailing wheels) for the largest express locomotives—in Britain, that is. There are larger ones elsewhere.

A tank locomotive carries its own water and coal supplies in tanks and bunker, instead of in a tender, and the wheel arrangement is followed by the letter T. The locomotive in the picture on p. 40 is a 2–4–0T, the tank formerly on the side nearest the photographer having been removed when she was sectioned. The usual position for water tanks is on either side of the boiler supported by the frames,

COMPONENTS OF A STEAM RAILWAY, AND HOW THEY WORK   43

21. (*opposite*) Basic design of goods rolling stock altered little throughout the steam railway era, though the variety of types was large, as this typical scene of the 1930s shows.

22. Late Victorian coaches—this one was built by the Midland Railway in 1885— were longer than those of earlier years, and often carried on six wheels, but still formed from separate compartments.

but a refinement of the system adds the letters ST to indicate a saddle tank locomotive on which the tank is carried, saddle fashion, on top of the boiler, and PT to indicate a pannier tank, with tanks slung one each side of the boiler like panniers. Tender locomotives were intended for long runs, tank locomotives for short runs and shunting.

Throughout the steam railway period, wagon design made little advance. Typically, open wagons had four wheels and wooden frames and sides, and were used for coal and other goods. Covered vans of similar construction were used for parcels and other traffic, partly open vans for cattle, and specialized types of wagons and vans for, for instance, timber, fruit, fish and oil.

The bodies of passenger carriages were originally similar to road coaches, mounted on four-wheeled wooden underframes like those of goods wagons. As longer coaches were designed, they were mounted on six wheels and later on two four-wheeled bogies. Bogies are pivoted so

23. Interior of a traditional signal box—this is Bewdley North, Severn Valley Railway. Levers operate points and signals, and telegraph instruments are on the shelf above.

that long coaches can pass round sharp curves, and they also make them ride more smoothly than four- and six-wheeled vehicles. By the end of the nineteenth century, express trains included bogie coaches with side corridors, corridor connections between them, dining-cars and sleeping-cars. Coach bodies were originally of wood, later of wood and steel; "all-steel" coaches were eventually introduced in the 1950s. The division of coaches into separate compartments originated with the practice of, in effect, putting several short road coach bodies on a single longer common underframe. The construction of compartment coaches ceased only some twenty years ago in favour of "open" coaches which can hold more people in the same area.

Automatic continuous brakes, operated by the driver and working on all the vehicles in a train (and coming on automatically on all of them if the train breaks in two) have been obligatory on passenger trains since 1889. But not on freight trains; hence the still familiar sight of the guard's van or brake van at the back of freight trains, where it provides braking power.

For safety, a railway line is divided up into "block sections" and only one train at a time is allowed in each section. Signalmen in signal boxes at the ends of each section communicate by telegraph to ensure that it is clear before allowing a train into it. Trains themselves are controlled by semaphore signals which, with the points, are worked by signalmen. The

COMPONENTS OF A STEAM RAILWAY, AND HOW THEY WORK

24. Some signals indicate not only whether a train may proceed but also by which route. At the approach to Wansford, Nene Valley Railway, the lower of the two signal arms, which is bracketed out to the left from the main post, has been "pulled off" to indicate that a train may take the track diverging to the left.

commonest types of signals are stop signals, with red arms, which indicate when horizontal that a train must stop, and when inclined up or down about forty-five degrees that it may proceed; and distant signals, with fish-tailed yellow arms, which give a driver advance warning of the indication of the next stop signal. At night, oil lamps light up coloured glasses attached to semaphore arms to give red, green or yellow indications. On modern railways, signals are electric colour lights, controlled from remote signal boxes, or automatically by trains themselves.

On double track railways, each track is normally used for trains in one direction only. On single track railways, an additional safeguard is the train staff or token. At its simplest, there is but one staff, usually a wood or metal rod, for each section between passing loops, and a driver may enter that section only if he has the staff—or, if another train is following, has been shown the staff by the signalman and given a ticket authorizing him to enter. Where single lines are busy—and on many preserved railways they are at times very busy indeed—the electric train staff system gives greater flexibility, allowing several trains in one direction to alternate with a few in the other, and so on. There are several "staffs" or "tablets" for each section, but they are kept in instruments, one at each end of the section, which are connected electrically so that only one staff can be removed from each pair of instruments at a time, and eventually replaced in either of them.

Chapter Four
OPERATION AND MAINTENANCE

Here is the scene at the main station of a typical preserved railway, around 10.00 am on a summer Saturday.

The air is still fresh, and passengers—plenty of them, but not such crowds as will appear later—are boarding the carriages standing at the platform. In due course a steam locomotive backs down on to the train and is coupled up. The guard blows his whistle and waves his green flag to give the "right away", and the first train of the day sets off.

This scene is not quite so simple as it at first appears. The first thing to remember is that most of the people running the railway, however professional they appear, are likely to be amateurs: volunteers who earn their livings elsewhere and come to the railway during their spare time and on holidays. On most preserved railways the volunteers present on an operating day probably outnumber the paid staff, even when the full-time staff are supplemented by temporary staff during the summer season, and by people employed under job creation schemes and the like.

To raise steam in a full-size locomotive takes about six hours from lighting the fire, if the locomotive is cold; if it has worked the previous day and is still warm, steam may be raised in four hours or so. Small narrow gauge locomotives take less time, two or three hours. But before a locomotive of any size is lit up, the grate must be cleared of ashes and clinker from the previous fire, and, most important, the level of water in the boiler must be checked and confirmed, by draining the gauge glasses and allowing them to re-fill, for too low a water level lets the firebox become dangerously hot. So preparing the locomotive on this summer Saturday begins at the latest around 7.30 am, and probably in the middle of the night.

While steam is being raised, the locomotive is cleaned and polished by cleaners and fireman, and when the driver comes on duty he "oils round"; that is, he works his way round the locomotive, oiling and checking the mechanical parts. Eventually the locomotive is ready to go to the train, and by that time much else has happened.

Next on the scene, after fireman and cleaners, are probably carriage cleaners, and then signalmen, who arrive about one

25. Locomotive cleaners on the Bluebell Railway clean and polish a South Eastern & Chatham Railway 0-6-0T of 1910.

and a half hours before the first train is due to depart. There may be shunting to be done, to put the right coaches in the right platform for the train, or a works train may be going out, to deliver replacement track materials to site, for instance. In both cases the motive power is likely to be a quick-starting diesel locomotive, the driver of which comes on duty about the same time as the signalman. Soon after them come booking clerks, car park attendants, and the staffs of gift shops and refreshment rooms. If the train includes buffet or restaurant cars, the people who are to run them arrive, take their supplies on board, check existing stocks and start preparing food. About one hour before the first train is due to leave, its guard comes on duty. He is in charge of the train: he must inspect it, make sure that it is clean and in order, check apparently obvious things such as that all the coaches are coupled together and, after the engine has been coupled on, check that the brakes are working.

As train time approaches, the signalman confirms by telegraph from the next box along the line that the section is clear,

26. The footplate of GWR 4-6-0 no. 7819 *Hinton Manor*, running on the Severn Valley Railway. The driver's left hand holds the regulator handle, the fireman shovels coal on to the fire.

extracts a train staff from the instrument and hands it to the driver; then he "pulls off" the appropriate signals to "clear". When the guard has checked from the station clock that it is indeed departure time, and made sure that all the doors are shut, he gives the driver the "right away": and only then does the train start.

Traditionally, there is a crew of two on a steam locomotive: driver and fireman. On preserved railways locomotives often have a crew of three, taking a cleaner as well—partly by way of reward for his cleaning efforts, and partly for him to learn how to fire a locomotive on the move. Fireman and cleaner share their tasks—the principal one being to ensure that the boiler produces the right amount of steam at the right times. This is done not merely by shovelling coal into the firebox—though ensuring that coal is fed to the fire when and where it is needed is itself a skilled task—but also by use of the fitting called the injector. The main purpose of this is to feed water into the boiler, replacing water used up as steam, but in doing so it reduces steam pressure. So to some extent it is also used by the skilled fireman to prevent steam pressure climbing too high—for when that happens steam blows off through the safety valves, wasting fuel and the fireman's work.

Fireman and cleaner are also likely to do jobs which on busier railways would be done by other staff—coupling and uncoupling the locomotive to and from the train, for instance, which would probably be done on BR by a shunter, and working lever frames and train staff instruments at stations which are unmanned.

The driver's principal controls are regulator handle, reversing lever (or wheel) and brake. The guard tells the driver when to start the train from stations, but how fast to go, and when to stop, are up to him—in accordance with signals, permanent and temporary speed restrictions, and timetable. He must be particularly alert for people on the track at level crossings: close to hand is a chain or wire to blow the whistle.

On the footplate of a locomotive, one is scarcely conscious of the train behind; but much is going on there. The guard keeps a look out to see that all is well; he can apply the brakes, if necessary. Travelling ticket inspectors inspect tickets and issue them to passengers who join at unstaffed stations. Buffet and restaurant car staff are busy serving drinks, snacks and meals. Several preserved railways have restaurant cars, and though their routes are not so long that meal service is essential, they are long enough for the novelty of a meal on a steam train to be enjoyed.

Typically a locomotive, with its train, makes three or four journeys up and down a preserved railway during the day, calling at intermediate stations and halts, crossing other trains at passing loops and taking water when necessary. At each terminus the locomotive runs round the train so as to be at the front. Crowds of passengers

27. Fireman's view of the Festiniog Railway from the cab of 2–6–2T *Mountaineer*. A chain supports the cab window, which has been hinged forward to lie horizontally.

OPERATION AND MAINTENANCE

28. Inside a preserved railway dining car: former International Sleeping Car Co. dining car no. 2975, on the Nene Valley Railway.

are greatest in the early afternoon and diminish again towards the end of the day (so when visiting a preserved railway it is always worth going in the morning or late afternoon if you can).

After the last train has arrived back at its terminus, the railway gradually closes down for the night. As with opening up in the morning, this is not an instant process. Cleaners go through the train, the guard

OPERATION AND MAINTENANCE 51

29. Volunteer signalman hands over train staff to locomotive crew as one train crosses another at Damems Loop, Worth Valley Railway.

reports any faults to the maintenance staff, signalmen, once shunting is completed, close their boxes, and staffs of booking office, buffet car and gift shops close down, and count their takings.

The crew of the locomotive, after uncoupling from the train, take her first to re-fill water tanks, and to re-load tender or bunker with coal ready for the next time she is steamed. Then the ashpan (beneath the firebox) and the smokebox must be emptied of ashes; the fire is probably left to burn out slowly, for to let a boiler cool down (or heat up) too quickly causes damage from contraction and expansion. Eventually, just enough steam pressure remains for the locomotive to move gently into the shed: the injector is put on for the last time, to knock the pressure back and fill up the boiler ready for the morning, and so the locomotive is settled down for the night.

By the standards of more modern machines, steam locomotives are inefficient and labour-intensive—that is to say, they use a lot of fuel and need a lot of looking after. They are also simple, robust and long-lived. They need frequent servicing—boiler tubes must be swept clean of clogging soot and ash, boilers themselves washed out to remove impurities. Mechanical parts need frequent examination, adjustment and replacement of worn

52 OPERATION AND MAINTENANCE

components. When steam was in regular use on BR, the largest express locomotives were stopped for servicing one day a week, and most others one day a fortnight.

Locomotives in preservation are generally used less intensively, and mechanical parts wear less quickly. Boilers, however, corrode at roughly the same rate whether used or not.

Carriages and wagons need comparatively little attention, though the wheels, bearings, couplings and brakes of those in daily use need examination every week or so, and paintwork also deteriorates at the same rate whether the vehicle is used or not, unless vehicles out of use are stored under cover.

All this has meant that preserved railways have had to set up extensive workshops where locomotives and coaches can be dismantled for their parts to be reconditioned, and subsequently re-erected; and since few lines which have been preserved had their own workshops, most of these have had to be set up from scratch.

Proper and continuous maintenance of the track is essential too, for it receives a continuous battering from passing trains. Loose keys have to be hammered home between chair and rail, track which has moved out of alignment crowbarred back into position. Ballast should enable rain-

30. Tender of LNER B1 class 4–6–0 is replenished with water at Loughborough, Great Central Railway.

31. (*opposite*) Steam locomotive maintenance: working inside the firebox of a BR standard class 4 4–6–0 on the Worth Valley Railway to renew boiler tubes.

OPERATION AND MAINTENANCE 53

water to drain away: if water starts to collect under a sleeper, the weight of passing trains pumps the sleeper up and down, rapidly making a hollow in the ballast beneath and causing a rough ride. So sleepers have to be "packed", by shovelling ballast beneath them to keep their levels correct, and lineside ditches have to be kept clear. Ballast itself eventually becomes mixed with earth and has to be replaced, and wooden sleepers rot and have to be renewed.

For every mile of route, a railway has to maintain in good order two miles of fences, one on each side, to prevent people and animals from straying on to it. And all the other components of a railway need constant attention and maintenance too—signals, telegraphs, bridges, viaducts, tunnels, and station buildings.

It has been the exception, rather than the rule, for preserved lines, when taken over by preservation groups, to be in first-class condition. Most experienced a period of disuse and partial dismantlement, so that it has been a long and arduous task to repair and where necessary reinstate track, signals and buildings.

32. Adjusting fishplate bolts (foreground) and crowbarring track into position on the Festiniog Railway's deviation.

Likewise, it has been rare for locomotives and rolling stock to enter preservation in good condition; usually extensive overhauls have been necessary, and locomotives recovered after many years in Barry scrapyard need several more years of loving attention to rebuild them into running order.

Adult volunteers, on one line or another, do almost all the tasks involved in operating, maintaining and restoring preserved railways and their equipment. For young people it is easiest to arrange to go to work as a volunteer on a preserved railway if you can go in the company of an adult—preferably a member of the preservation society concerned—who already does so, or else as one of an organized group such as Scouts or school parties. It is I regret to say not easy for anyone under sixteen years old without such an introduction to go independently to work voluntarily on a preserved railway. This restriction is largely a safety measure. The main concern of any railway is safety, particularly the safety of passengers. The potential on railways for accidents from simple causes is immense: it ranges from the truly serious—a bad derailment, say, with people killed or injured, caused by sleepers and tools left lying about on the track—to the near-comic—a can of paint spilt over someone's trousers, perhaps (but the platform that was deserted when you started to paint the fence may quickly have become crowded when a train was due, and it is not so funny for the wearer of the trousers, whether that is a waiting passenger or yourself).

So everyone working on a railway should know the dangers likely to arise and cause accidents, and the precautions to take against them. Anyone who does not must work under the supervision of someone responsible who does. The insurance policies of some preserved railways restrict them to volunteers aged sixteen or over.

Despite these restrictions, many people under sixteen do work voluntarily in railway preservation; they enjoy themselves, and they make a useful contribution. A line which encourages volunteers to come in family parties is the Nene Valley Railway. Young volunteers, boys and girls, work with adults as assistant guards, as assistant travelling ticket inspectors, on the locomotives, and in the booking office, restaurant car and gift shop. Other tasks done by junior members of preservation societies (on the Nene Valley and elsewhere) include helping in refreshment rooms, signal boxes and car parks, helping to keep stations and carriages clean and tidy, painting buildings and signs and such like.

As juniors assist older members doing more complex tasks, they gradually gain the experience needed to do those tasks themselves. Locomotive-cleaning is the first step on the road to firing and, in due course, driving. And cleaning a locomotive has more point than just making it look smart: there is no better way of familiarizing yourself with all the details of a locomotive than cleaning it all over. Further, in the course of being cleaned, worn or damaged parts are discovered before they break.

56 OPERATION AND MAINTENANCE

33. (*opposite*) Volunteer guard and assistant give the "Right Away" on the Nene Valley Railway.

Participants in organized groups find themselves doing most of the tasks just mentioned, and others where many hands make light work. These include cutting back bushes, trees and undergrowth where they have grown too near the track, digging out and clearing away the grass and debris covering disused track which it is intended to reinstate, and clearing and levelling the ground for new sidings.

Notable among the many school parties which help preserved railways are those from Chace School, Enfield, Middlesex, which travel to North Wales to help on the Festiniog Railway under the school's senior master Mr Keith Catchpole, and those from Norham High School, North Shields, which help on the Bowes Railway nearby under the school's head of history, Mr Colin Mountford. Chace School working parties (they are known to friends as The Tadpoles) have been a familiar and valued part of the Festiniog scene since the 1950s and about 1,300 boys have now taken part in them. The Norham school parties, as well as doing jobs of the types mentioned above, make a speciality of repairs to wagons (primarily their axleboxes and brakes, and repainting them). A unique feature of the Bowes Railway is its operation of steep inclines by rope haulage, that is to say hauling wagons up, and lowering them down, by rope from a winding engine at the top. This technique was much used on railways built before the 1840s but is now almost extinct, and to demonstrate it sets of wagons have to be maintained.

Chapter Five

MUSEUMS, DEPOTS AND MAIN LINE STEAM

This chapter and the next indicate where steam locomotives and all the things that go with them may still be seen and enjoyed in preservation. The two chapters are not wholly comprehensive: to attempt this would be to reduce them to lists so condensed as to be useless. For a comprehensive guide to what locomotives, and so on, are in which museum or on which preserved railway, with addresses, it is best to refer to an annual publication such as *Railways Restored*. This is the official yearbook of the Association of Railway Preservation Societies and is published by Ian Allan Ltd.

The principal museum of science and technology in the British Isles is the Science Museum, London, and so its immense collection includes important early locomotives, notably Hedley's *Puffing Billy* (1814) and the Stephensons' *Rocket* (1829). *Rocket* was much modified after the Rainhill Trials (see page 15), to take advantage of later developments in locomotive design, so a full-size non-working replica of her in Rainhill condition is exhibited nearby. Nearby too is the original *Sans Pareil*; across the aisle

MUSEUMS, DEPOTS AND MAIN LINE STEAM 59

from these historic machines stands GWR 4–6–0 *Caerphilly Castle* of 1923, a good representative of steam express power at its greatest, as shown on this page and the next.

34. Locomotives at the Science Museum, London: on the left, from the front, *Puffing Billy*, *Rocket*, *Sans Pareil*, and a later industrial tank locomotive; on the right, GWR express 4–6–0 *Caerphilly Castle*.

Among many other displays the most interesting is that of instructional models of locomotive valve gears. By turning the handles one can see almost immediately how the valve admits steam to the cylinder and releases it, and by adjusting the reversing lever how altering valve positions reverses the engine. These things are extraordinarily hard to follow from a written description, or even from diagrams.

The fundamentals of the steam railway can be studied at the Science Museum, London, but you must go to its out-station at York, the National Railway Museum, to find locomotives, coaches and other equipment displayed in all the varieties of style, size, shape and colour that were typical of the railway companies of the steam railway era. The Great Western, for instance, was noted for its chocolate-and-cream coaches and its dark green locomotives with copper-capped chimneys, and the London & North Western painted its locomotives a deep and lustrous black. Painstaking restoration of locomotives and rolling stock to their original liveries is a feature of railway preservation, not only at the NRM but also elsewhere.

The National Railway Museum is the principal home of the national collection of preserved locomotives and other railway equipment, but the main building, though large, cannot contain the whole of it. Some items are rotated between the main building and the reserve collection, some are loaned to other responsible railway preservation groups, some locomotives go forth from the museums to haul steam specials. The workable replica of *Rocket*, built in 1980, belongs to the NRM but is often away working elsewhere.

35. *Caerphilly Castle* enters Patchway, near Bristol, with a GWR express from South Wales to London. This locomotive is now in the Science Museum.

MUSEUMS, DEPOTS AND MAIN LINE STEAM 61

36. Record breakers in the National Railway Museum. *Hardwicke*, on the left, ran the 141 miles from Crewe to Carlisle at an *average* speed of 67.2 mph in 1895. *Mallard* is on the right.

Always, however, the National Railway Museum contains a nucleus of the notable and the typical. The most famous exhibit, and probably the most visited, is *Mallard*, the LNER streamlined 4–6–2 of the unbroken 126 mph speed record for steam. The collection of royal coaches with authentic period interiors gives an insight into the luxury provided for travelling royalty, particularly Queen Victoria. This museum has the best selection of Victorian and Edwardian steam locomotives

37. (*opposite*) The sumptuous interior of Queen Victoria's saloon can now be seen in the National Railway Museum.

in existence; it includes *Gladstone*, mentioned in Chapter 2. One of the tracks upon which locomotives stand has a deep and illuminated pit between the rails, into which visitors descend to view those working parts of a locomotive usually hidden between the main frames. One locomotive—SR 4-6-2 *Ellerman Lines*—is sectioned so that the interiors of firebox, boiler, smokebox and cylinder can be seen. One of the other locomotives—in 1981 it was LSWR 4-4-0 no. 563, built in 1893—has steps positioned so that visitors can go on to the footplate. The museum's education service arranges visits for about 600 school parties each year.

The Great Western Railway Museum, Swindon, houses many national collection items relating to the GWR. They include the famous 4-4-0 *City of Truro*, which in 1904 ran the seventy-five miles from Exeter to Bristol at an average of over 70 mph and probably reached a maximum of over 102 mph in the process. At that date motor cars could run legally at 20 mph, illegally a little faster. The museum contains four other representative GWR locomotives and many smaller relics.

General transport museums containing important railway exhibits include Glasgow Museum of Transport with four locomotives and other equipment from Scottish railways, and the London Transport Museum with a Metropolitan Railway 4-4-0T built in 1866, of the type used on London underground lines before they were electrified. Many operating preserved railways have museums, either of general interest such as the Narrow Gauge Railway Museum at the Talyllyn Railway's Tywyn Wharf station, or of specific local interest such as the Festiniog Railway's museum at Porthmadog Harbour station.

Elsewhere disused stations have become railway museums. Notable is Manchester, Liverpool Road, the original Manchester terminus of the Liverpool & Manchester Railway. It still includes the original buildings of 1830 and is being adapted to house the North Western Museum of Science & Industry. The station building of Monkwearmouth station, Sunderland (a fine piece of classical architecture) now houses much of the Land Transport Collection of Tyne &

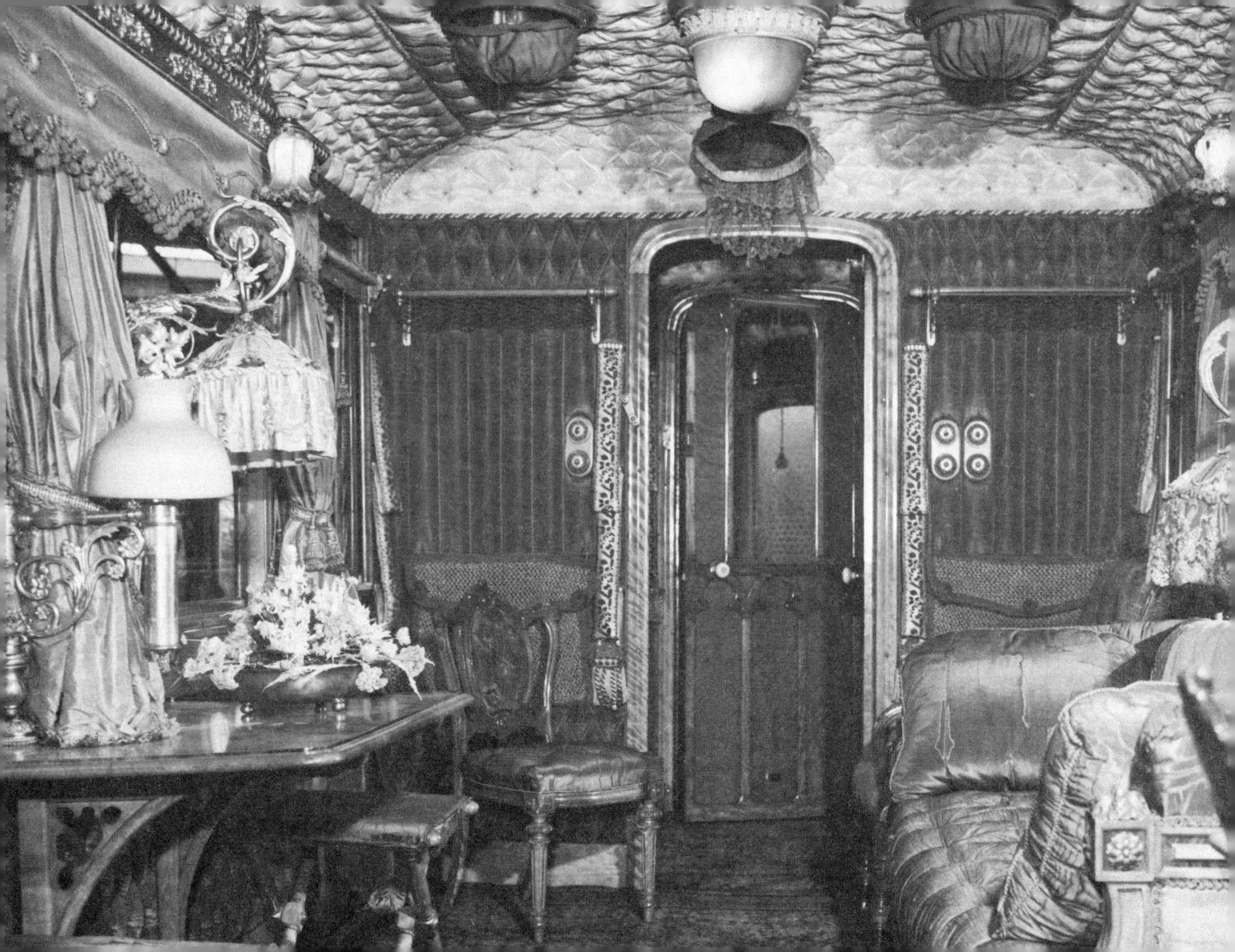

64 MUSEUMS, DEPOTS AND MAIN LINE STEAM

38. Monkwearmouth station is said to have been given an ornate and imposing building to mark the election of George Hudson, railway tycoon of the 1840s, as MP for neighbouring Sunderland. Today it is Monkwearmouth Station Museum.

Wear County Museums service. At Wolferton, once the station for Sandringham, part of the station building has become a museum devoted to travel by royal train.

All these stations are wholly closed, but Darlington, North Road, remains open as a paytrain halt. It is much larger than is necessary for present-day traffic, and most of it is converted into North Road Station Railway Museum. Its most famous exhibit is, as mentioned in Chapter 2, *Locomotion*.

Other locomotives, rolling stock and small exhibits relate to the Stockton & Darlington Railway, the NER, and other railways of North East England.

Close beside the line of the Stockton & Darlington Railway at Shildon is the Timothy Hackworth Museum. Hackworth was the S & DR's first locomotive superintendent, with the task of making the Stephensons' none-too-successful locomotives work while the Stephensons themselves were away building railways elsewhere. The museum is the house in which he lived; partly re-furnished in contemporary manner, it displays exhibits of his life and times. He built *Sans Pareil* for the Rainhill Trials, and so a locomotive shed nearby, once part of his works, is now the home of the working replica of *Sans Pareil* built in 1980.

A working replica of Trevithick's 1804 locomotive was completed in 1981 for the Welsh Industrial & Maritime Museum, Cardiff, and is steamed there from time to time. The replica of *Locomotion* built in 1975 can often be seen working at Beamish North of England Open Air Museum, Co. Durham. At Beamish the past way of life

MUSEUMS, DEPOTS AND MAIN LINE STEAM 65

39. Rowley station, North Eastern Railway, was reconstructed within Beamish North of England Open Air Museum in the mid-1970s.

of North East England is being re-created in all its many aspects from coal mining to cooking. So a new working steam railway is being constructed, which re-uses authentic locomotives, rolling stock, track, signals and buildings. The latter, such as Rowley station, have been carefully taken down at their original sites and re-erected within the museum.

What the Beamish museum is doing for North East England, the Midland Railway Trust Ltd is doing for the Midland Railway. It has acquired an immense collection of equipment of Midland and LMS origin, from locomotives and signal boxes to small relics and engineering drawings. The trust has also acquired part of the closed Midland Railway branch line from Ambergate to Pye Bridge, near Derby, and here the Midland Railway Centre is being developed. Eventually there will be an extensive museum under cover and a demonstration line three and a half miles long with several stations. The line, of which little was left but the track, is being re-equipped and the stations rebuilt (the most important, at the time of writing, is Butterley) with authentic MR materials.

40. Restored LMS 0–6–0T no. 7298 and an inspection saloon provide train rides at Steamport Transport Museum, Southport.

The day before I wrote this, the timetable for the opening of the operating line reached me.

At preservation depots locomotives and rolling stock are restored and maintained, and displayed to the public. Most of them also offer train rides for passengers over short distances—up and down a siding, say; such depots are often also called museums or railway centres. The most fortunate are those which are also the bases for preserved locomotives hauling steam specials over British Rail lines.

It is at Steamtown Railway Museum, Carnforth, that the appearance of the pre-1968 steam depot is most nearly recreated, when locomotives are being prepared for the steam specials worked from here—round the coast to Ravenglass and Sellafield, inland to Hellifield and York, and over the scenic Settle & Carlisle line. The main building at Steamtown is a locomotive running shed built only in the 1940s and typical of its period. It retains much of its original track layout, its turntable, and its mechanical coaling and ash

MUSEUMS, DEPOTS AND MAIN LINE STEAM 67

disposal plants. Even so, it is unusual for more than three locomotives to be in steam at Carnforth at the same time; in the old days there might have been ten times as many.

Steam workings between Didcot, Stratford upon Avon and the outskirts of Birmingham are shared between Didcot Railway Centre and Birmingham Railway Museum, Tyseley. Didcot Railway Centre is operated by the Great Western Society, which specializes in the preservation of relics of the GWR and has an extensive and excellent collection of its locomotives and coaches. The centre itself is based on and around the former locomotive shed at Didcot.

41. (*top*) Southern Railway 4–6–0 *Lord Nelson* leaves Skipton, Yorkshire, with a steam special over BR in 1980.

42. The Great Western Society's Didcot Railway Centre is based on the former GWR locomotive shed at Didcot, Oxfordshire.

43. (*opposite*) LMS 4–6–2 *Duchess of Hamilton* leaves York with *The Limited Edition* steam special over BR in May 1980. This run marked the locomotive's return to working order after an interval of seventeen years.

Other bases for steam workings over BR include the Bulmer Railway Centre, Hereford, from which GWR 4–6–0 *King George V* and other famous locomotives work between Newport, Hereford, Shrewsbury and Chester; Dinting Railway Centre at Glossop, Derbyshire, noted for two LMS Jubilee class locomotives *Bahamas* and *Leander*; and the NRM itself, whence exhibits such as LMS 4–6–2 *Duchess of Hamilton* emerge to work steam trains to Scarborough and elsewhere. Locomotives and coaches of the Scottish Railway Preservation Society, based on its depot at Falkirk, are able to work over many of the lines in the vicinity, along with the privately-owned streamlined 4–6–2 *Union of South Africa*, which was built by the LNER.

Preserved steam locomotives intended to run over British Rail are stringently inspected by BR, and the number of those passed to do so is few—usually about thirty at any one time. Locomotives recently overhauled are sometimes added to the list, and those needing overhaul removed from it for the time being. The routes over which they may run are also varied year by year, but usually total about 1,000 miles. Regular BR-sponsored steam excursions are detailed in the BR annual timetable; for details of other steam excursions over BR it is best to consult the "Coming Events" pages of the *Railway Magazine* and other railway journals.

These pages also include details of steam specials in Ireland. The Railway Preservation Society of Ireland has enjoyed better co-operation over steam specials from the two Irish railway systems, *Coras Iompair Eireann* and Northern Ireland Railways, than have British societies from British Rail; although, to be fair, Irish railways tend to be less busy than those in Britain. There was never a steam ban in Ireland and special trains of RPSI locomotives and, in some instances, coaches, based on its depot at Whitehead, Co. Antrim, have traversed at one time or another the entire surviving Irish railway network.

There are in Britain some other notable preservation depots which do not, because of their locations, provide locomotives to run over BR. Among them are Bressingham Steam Museum, near Diss, Norfolk,

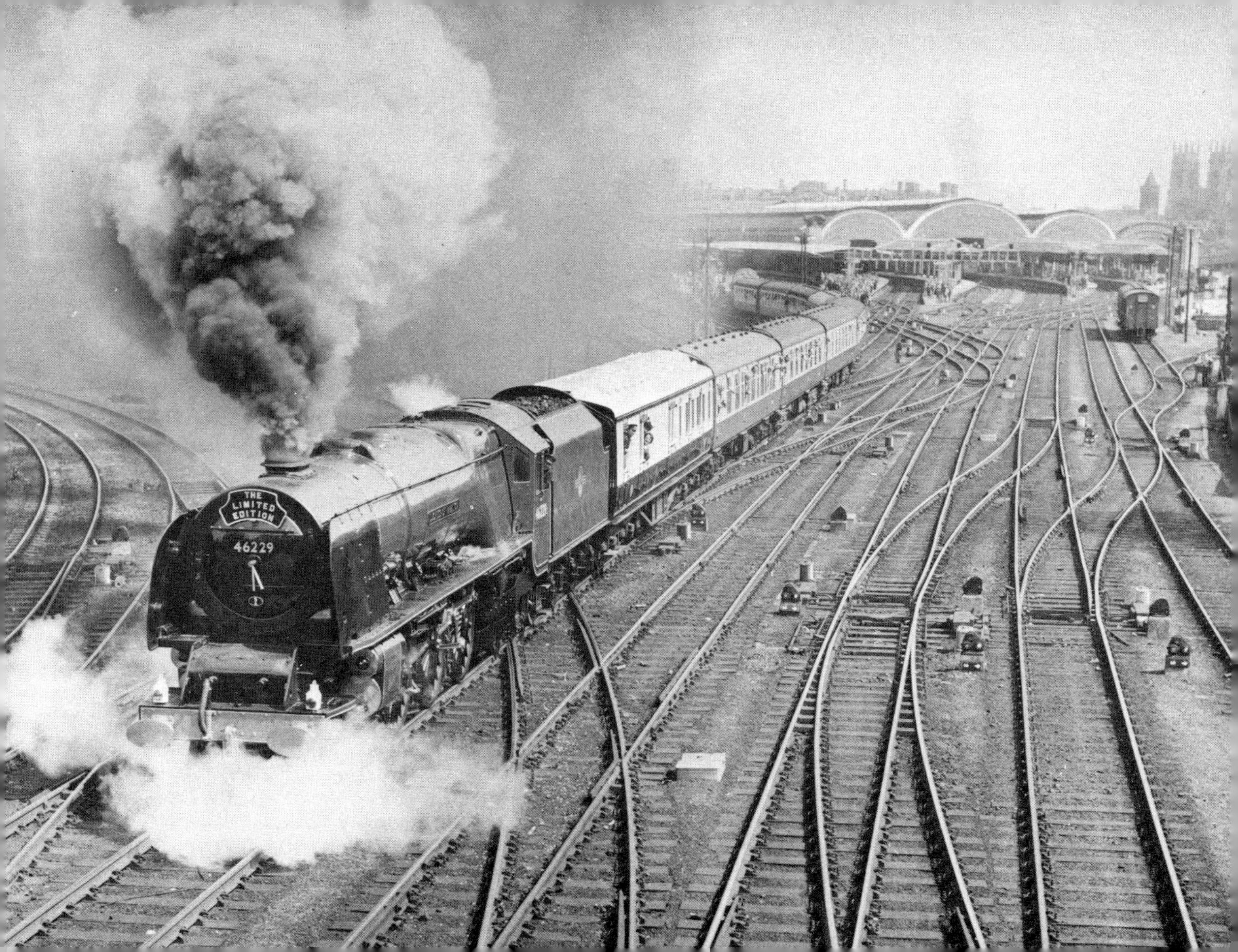
THE LIMITED EDITION
46229

built up from nothing by its originator Alan Bloom and now with railways of four different gauges; the old-established depots of the Dowty Railway Preservation Society (Ashchurch, Glos.) and the Quainton Railway Society Ltd (Quainton, Bucks), and the more recent Steamport Transport Museum, Southport. All these have extensive collections of working locomotives and rolling stock. Elsewhere such depots have often been set up as a first step towards hoped-for preservation of a branch line: Norchard Steam Centre near Lydney, Glos., is an example at the time of writing, and many of the lines described in the next chapter started in this way.

44. (*top*) A Railway Preservation Society of Ireland special pauses at Rathduff, on the CIE Cork–Dublin main line. Locomotives are Great Southern & Western Railway 0–6–0 no. 186 and Great Northern Railway (Ireland) 4–4–0 *Slieve Gullion*; firemen of both have climbed up to shift coal forward in the tenders.

45. The *Portrush Flyer*, formed from a locomotive and coaches of the Railway Preservation Society of Ireland, runs on several Saturdays each summer over Northern Ireland Railways between Belfast and the seaside resort of Portrush.

Chapter Six
THE PRINCIPAL PRESERVED RAILWAYS

Museums of the traditional type enable unique historic relics to be preserved intact, indefinitely, but static. Steam preservation depots enable locomotives and coaches to be not only preserved but operated for the public, and since distances are limited, their mechanical parts do not wear out quickly. Steam specials over main lines perpetuate the spectacle of steam locomotives running fast and working hard, and the experience of travelling long distances behind steam. But each of these aspects of railway preservation has limitations. One can gain an insight into all the workings of a steam railway only by visiting, or better still working on, a preserved operating line.

Preserved railways do not run trains every day. Those near big towns and cities usually operate at weekends throughout most of the year; during the week they operate less frequently and only at the height of summer. Those in holiday areas run daily from spring until autumn and are busiest on high summer weekdays. Once again, the best detailed reference is an annual guide such as *Railways Restored* which includes timetables.

46. The Talyllyn Railway is now busy and well-maintained, in marked contrast to its state in the early 1950s.

The Talyllyn Railway has now functioned as a preserved railway for over thirty years. When it was first preserved, steam locomotives were an everyday sight, and did not provide the main motive for preserving the TR. Its attractions were three: the historic nature of its locomotives and coaches, which were even then over eighty years old (the usual working life of a steam locomotive was about half this); the appeal of its less-than-full-size narrow gauge trains, particularly at a time when most narrow gauge lines had closed; and the fact that it was still owned by one of the very, very few original railway companies to have escaped both amalgamation and nationalization. Those three features are still present on the Talyllyn, but other things have changed. In 1951 it was utterly ramshackle, but now it is well equipped and maintained. The rapid increase in passenger traffic meant that the renewal of the track, the overhaul of locomotives and rolling stock, the addition of four more steam locomotives, and the construction of many new coaches have been essential. The route remains the same and attractive as ever, running inland from Wharf Station at Tywyn (Gwynedd) to Abergynolwyn, the original passenger terminus, and onward for three-quarters of a mile, over route formerly used only by goods trains, to a new terminus at Nant Gwernol.

Those three features of the Talyllyn —historic equipment, narrow gauge, original company—were features also of the Festiniog Railway, with the difference that in the early 1950s the FR, once a small-scale main line far busier than the TR, had degenerated far more. Since its closure in 1946 its route among the Welsh mountains from Porthmadog to Blaenau Ffestiniog had become in places so overgrown that one could not walk along it. And soon after Alan Pegler obtained control, but before any of it had been re-opened, an Act of Parliament allowed part of the course of the railway to be submerged by a new reservoir needed for a hydro-electric scheme.

So the Festiniog Railway has been recovering from dereliction and re-opened by stages, since 1955. To an even greater extent than the Talyllyn it has seen a rapid increase in numbers of passengers, which

47. (*opposite*) In early spring, Festiniog Railway *Prince* and train encounter snow on the deviation route built to avoid the reservoir in the background.

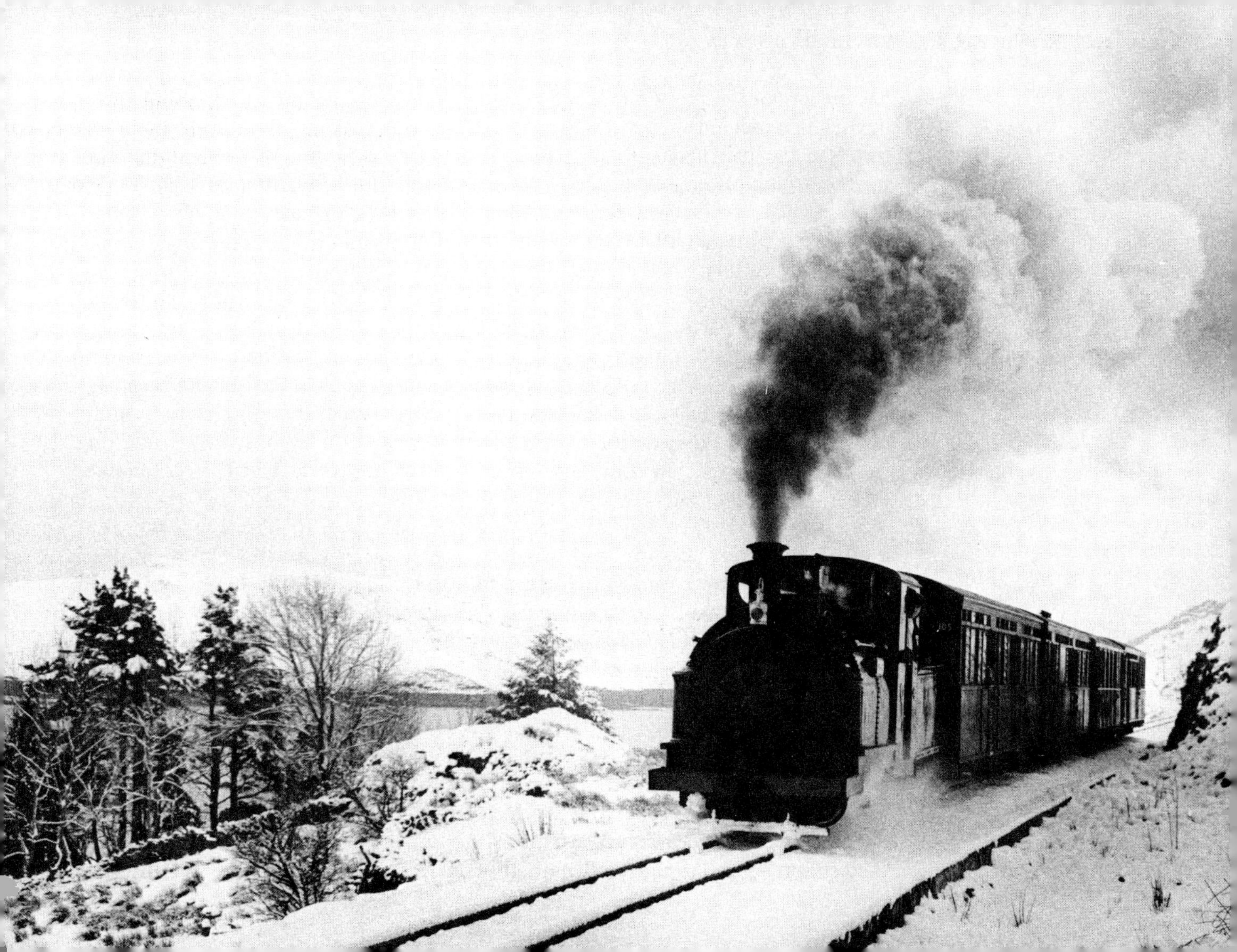

has meant not only rebuilding and repairing original locomotives and rolling stock but also the provision of more and improved locomotives, many new coaches, re-laid track, and reinstated signalling, telephone and telegraph systems. Among the historic rolling stock are the first two bogie coaches built in Britain (in 1872). Locomotives of particular interest include 0–4–0T *Prince*, originally supplied in 1863 and many times rebuilt, and two double Fairlie 0–4–4–0Ts. Locomotives of this powerful type, double-ended like two locomotives back to back, and carried on bogies, were adopted by the FR in the 1860s to solve its problem of conveying heavy loads over narrow and winding track. The two now running are *Merddin Emrys*, built originally in 1879 and many times rebuilt, and *Earl of Merioneth*, a new locomotive on the old principle completed by the FR in 1979 and incorporating parts of older locomotives.

To avoid the flooded section, a deviation line two and three-quarter miles long was built between 1965 and 1978, much of it by volunteers. It commences at Dduallt station with a spiral, unique in Britain: the line gains height by climbing through a loop, crossing over itself by a bridge, before regaining its original direction at a higher level. Further on it passes through a tunnel 294 yards long. This deviation is the most ambitious civil engineering project ever undertaken by a preserved railway. From 1978 to 1981, the trains from Porthmadog terminated at Tanygrisiau where the deviation re-joins the original route. The final section into Blaenau Ffestiniog was being restored and was reopened on 25 May 1982, marking the 150th anniversary of the company.

Passenger trains of the 2 ft. 6 in. gauge Welshpool & Llanfair Light Railway once again reached the first of its name towns in 1981. This is a genuine light railway, built under a light railway order of 1899, all ups and downs with sharp curves and steep gradients. After its closure by British Railways in 1956 a preservation society was formed, and the western part of the line, from Llanfair Caereinion (Powys) to Castle Caereinion, was eventually reopened as a preserved line in 1963; train services were extended to Sylfaen in 1972. The section thence to Welshpool, re-

THE PRINCIPAL PRESERVED RAILWAYS 75

48. A train of the Welshpool & Llanfair Light Railway ascends Golfa bank on 9 August 1981, three weeks after this section had been re-opened to passengers after an interval of fifty years. The 2–6–2T no. 14 was built for the Sierra Leone Railways as recently as 1954.

opened in 1981, is very steeply graded; in places as steep as 1 in 29: it is not often that you see the railway carriage in which you are sitting tilted on end by the gradient. The railway still has the two original locomotives built for it in 1902, but the original passenger coaches were scrapped long ago. Present-day trains are often made up of coaches obtained from Austria and Sierra Leone, hauled by an imported locomotive, though two of these, obtained from Antigua in the West Indies and from Sierra Leone, were British-built, as were the Sierra Leone coaches.

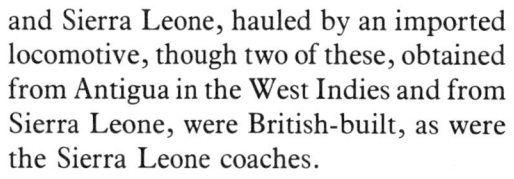

The success of preserved narrow gauge lines in Wales has prompted the construction of the Bala Lake Railway and the Brecon Mountain Railway, both of them built to gauges slightly less than 2 ft. on the courses of closed British Railways lines, and the Llanberis Lake Railway, similarly built on the course of a dismantled industrial line. All use preserved steam locomotives. The Snowdon Mountain Railway, the rack railway up Snowdon, continues to operate, unpreserved, with steam locomotives, and so does British Rail's 1 ft. $11\frac{1}{2}$ in. gauge Vale of Rheidol line from Aberystwyth to Devil's Bridge.

The 3 ft. gauge system of the Isle of Man Railway was built in the 1870s. It survived as a commercial railway until as late as 1965; subsequently it, or part of it, has been operated with voluntary support as a preserved line for tourist traffic. In 1977 the Douglas to Port Erin line, fifteen and a half miles long (the only section surviving)

was taken over by the Manx government and now forms part of Isle of Man Railways, along with the vintage Manx Electric Railway. The steam railway is operated with several attractive 2–4–0Ts, survivors of a larger fleet once operated by the railway company; the coaches too are originals.

In England few narrow gauge lines were built, and one of those few, the 3 ft. gauge Ravenglass & Eskdale, closed in 1913 after the closure of the mines and quarries it served. But from 1915 onwards the track was re-laid by 1 ft. 3 in. gauge and the line re-opened as a miniature railway: that is, it was deliberately made small to attract passengers, and the locomotives were models, with the proportion of full-size locomotives scaled down to match the track. In this form it was for some years much more successful, but once again faced closure and dismantling in 1960, when it was put up for sale by auction.

49. *Northern Rock*, built in 1975, enters Ravenglass station on the 1 ft. 3 in. gauge Ravenglass & Eskdale Railway.

Happily it was purchased for preservation and has since, with voluntary support, been busier and more prosperous than ever. Increasing traffic has meant construction of two new steam locomotives, 2-8-2 *River Mite* in 1966 and 2-6-2 *Northern Rock* in 1975. *Northern Rock* has the proportions of a narrow gauge rather than model locomotive and the railway as a whole no longer emphasizes the miniature aspect. The line runs among the hills of the Lake District for seven miles from Ravenglass inland to Eskdale (Dalegarth).

In the south of England the counterpart of the R&ER is the Romney Hythe & Dymchurch Railway, built during the 1920s to 1 ft. 3 in. gauge. Many of its locomotives are miniatures of the 4-6-2 express locomotives of the period between the wars, and they haul long trains of bogie coaches over its double track main line across Romney Marsh. In 1972 the line was threatened with closure because much of its equipment was old and worn, but it was purchased by a group of railway enthusiasts headed by W. H. McAlpine and assisted by a supporters' association. The railway runs for fourteen miles along the south coast of Kent, from Hythe through New Romney to Dungeness.

To turn now to standard gauge lines, the Bluebell Railway, as mentioned on page 32, was the first former-BR line to be re-opened as a preserved railway, in 1960. Being early in the field it was able to build up a unique collection of pre-grouping tank locomotives suitable for hauling trains on its five-mile line. More recently it has acquired some newer and larger locomotives, but nearly all formerly worked in the south of England, mostly on the Southern Railway or its constituents. So, too, did most of the coaches. With many of the locomotives and coaches restored to their former liveries, the appearance of south-of-England trains from times past is convincingly recreated.

Trains run by the Severn Valley Railway between Bewdley and Bridgnorth appear to be those of the GWR, the LMS, or pre-modernization British Railways: authentic locomotives and complete trains of authentic coaches have been restored and repainted in their correct colours. Their twelve-and-three-quarter mile route was formerly part of the Great Western

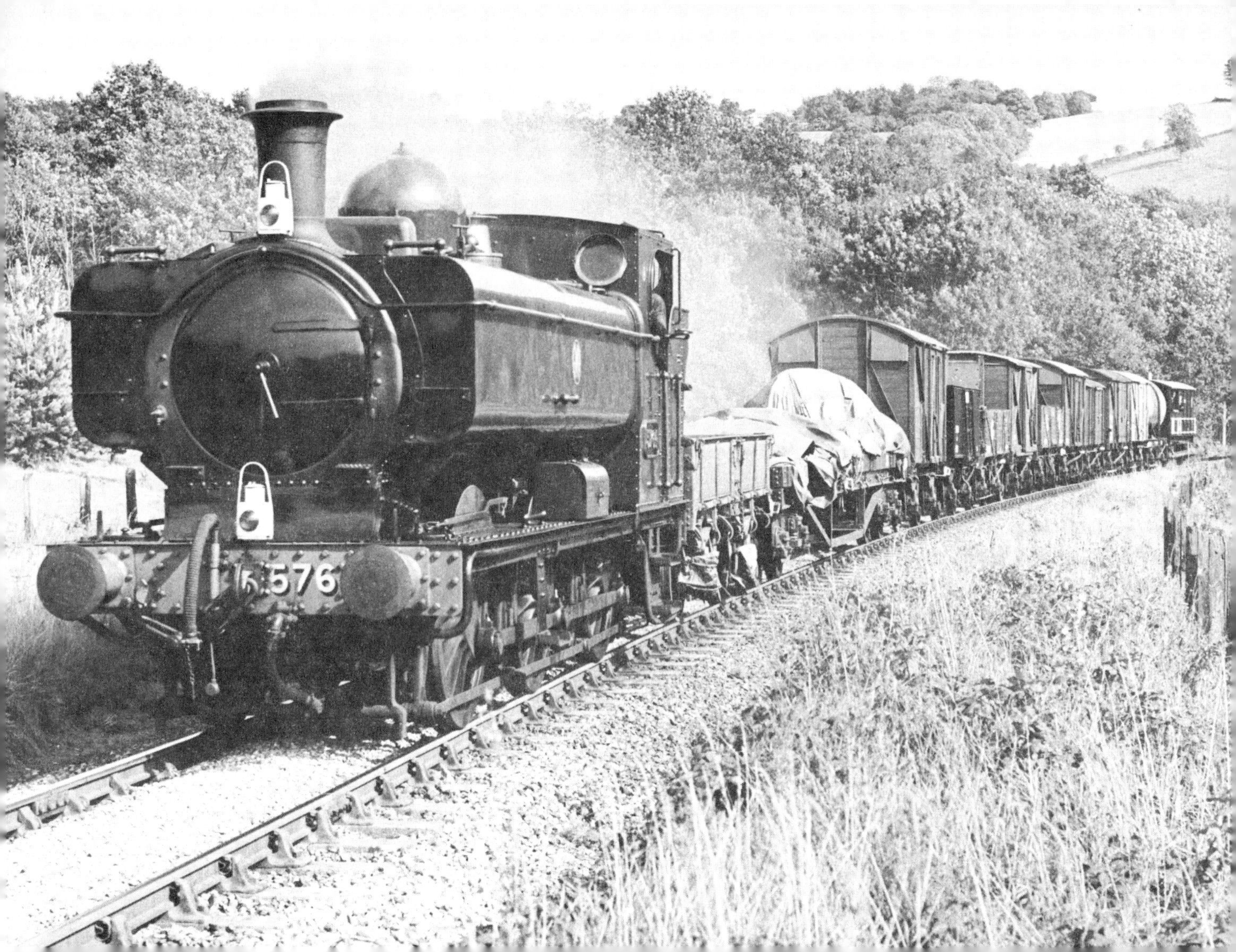
576

50. (*opposite*) On an enthusiasts' day in 1980 the Severn Valley Railway re-creates a steam-age mixed goods train with preserved locomotive and rolling stock.

Shrewsbury–Worcester line. It was closed to passengers in 1963 and re-opened between 1970 and 1974. As well as passenger trains, both the Bluebell and Severn Valley Railways from time to time run complete trains of preserved goods rolling stock, to re-create the appearance of steam-age goods trains for the benefit of onlookers—and photographers.

The two lines of the Dart Valley Railway—Buckfastleigh and Torbay—also have a Great Western appearance. Restored GWR locomotives haul trains of coaches in GWR chocolate-and-cream. Some of these coaches are original GWR stock, some are early BR coaches repainted. Many preserved railways use BR coaches built in the 1950s for their busiest holiday trains, to save wear and tear on more historic vehicles; painting them in GWR colours has a precedent, for BR's Western Region did just this to some of its coaches at one time.

The Buckfastleigh line is part of the former GWR branch line from Totnes, Devon, to Buckfastleigh and Ashburton. This was closed to passengers in 1958 and goods in 1962. The Dart Valley Light Railway Ltd was formed to re-open it as a steam line, with a supporters' association. But it was unable to re-open all of it: at one end, the site of the Buckfastleigh to Ashburton section was needed for a road improvement scheme, and at the other, Dart Valley trains are not permitted to enter Totnes BR station, for to do so they would have to cross the River Dart bridge and therefore to run for a short distance along the Paddington–Penzance main line. In 1969 the DVR re-opened the branch from Buckfastleigh for six and a half miles to Totnes Riverside, a run-round loop just short of the main line junction and without public access except by train. Thwarted in much of its original intention, the Dart Valley company jumped at the chance of purchasing the Paignton–Kingswear line when this was to be closed by BR in 1972: and train services, for once, continued without interruption at the takeover.

The Keighley & Worth Valley Railway Preservation Society was more fortunate than the DVR when it sought to re-open the former Midland Railway branch line which runs for four and three-quarter

THE PRINCIPAL PRESERVED RAILWAYS

51. A Paignton-to-Kingswear train of the Dart Valley Railway's Torbay line approaches Churston in 1980, hauled by a GWR 2-6-2T.

miles from Keighley, West Yorkshire, to Haworth and Oxenhope. This was closed by BR in 1962. The branch had its own platform at Keighley, which trains could reach without conflicting with the Leeds–Carlisle main line—so, when it was re-opened in 1968 as the Worth Valley Railway, it was re-opened complete from end to end.

Busy preserved-railway traffic soon needed frequent trains, so a half-way passing loop was installed in 1971, controlled in due course by a Midland Railway signal box recovered from near Bradford.

THE PRINCIPAL PRESERVED RAILWAYS 81

52. North York Moors Railway train approaches Goathland with 0-6-2T no. 5, which was built in 1909 for Lambton, Hetton & Joicey Collieries Ltd's industrial railway.

Locomotives on the Worth Valley Railway include the Midland Railway 4F class 0-6-0 which was the first locomotive rescued from Barry scrapyard, but in general, like many other preserved railways, it does not attempt to reproduce the appearance of any particular bygone company. Rather, its large collection of locomotives is extremely diverse both in size, from the smallest to the largest types, and in origin, for LMS, LNER, GWR, Southern, and BR are all represented. Perhaps the most interesting, however, is the S160 class 2-8-0 nicknamed *Big Jim*. Many locomotives of this class were built in the USA during the Second World War and worked for a year or two on Britain's hard-pressed railways before being shipped to the Continent after the invasion. The Worth Valley example was eventually recovered from Poland, behind the Iron Curtain, in 1977.

So each preserved railway has its own character. The North Yorkshire Moors Railway offers an eighteen-mile ride by steam or diesel train between Grosmont and Pickering, over a route which dates from the 1830s and now gives access to the North York Moors National Park. The Kent & East Sussex Railway from Tenterden to Wittersham Road is part of an original light railway. The Great Central Railway from Loughborough to Rothley, Leicestershire, is a section of former main line, that of the old Great Central Railway from London (Marylebone) to Sheffield and Manchester. The North Norfolk Railway, Sheringham to Weybourne, is a section of the former Midland & Great Northern Joint Railway, a joint attempt by the two companies of its name to compete with the Great Eastern for traffic to Norfolk seaside resorts.

53. LNER B1 class 4–6–0 runs round its train at Rothley, Great Central Railway.

54. (*opposite*) A traffic jam enables motorists to admire a train of the North Norfolk Railway en route from Sheringham to Weybourne.

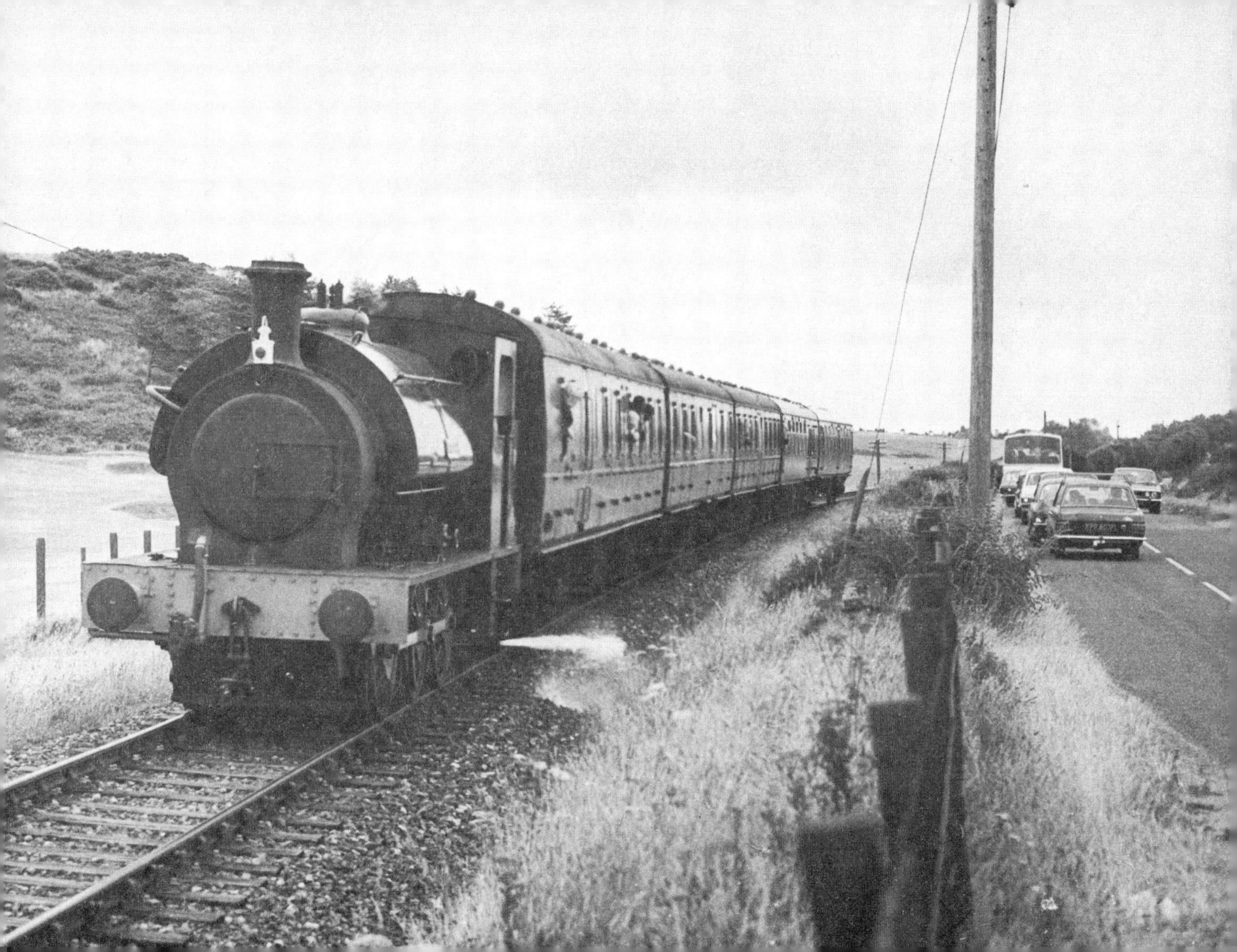

The Lakeside & Haverthwaite Railway in Cumbria was prevented by road improvements from connecting with BR trains, but it does connect at Lakeside with motor vessels which BR still operates on Lake Windermere. The Nene Valley Railway, from Peterborough (Orton Mere) to Wansford specializes in Continental locomotives and rolling stock, but it also provides a home for 4–6–2 *Britannia*, the first British Railways standard steam locomotive to be built, in 1951. Several preserved railways provide a steam presence in parts of Britain where it would otherwise be absent. These include the Strathspey Railway from Aviemore to Boat of Garten in the Scottish Highlands, the Gwili Railway from Bronwydd Arms to Penybont, near Carmarthen in South Wales, and the Isle of Wight Steam Railway from Haven Street to Wootton. The Mid-Hants Railway (Alresford to Ropley) and the West Somerset Railway (Minehead to Bishop's Lydeard) are both recent successes which have arisen out of particularly controversial closures of branch lines by BR.

All these standard gauge lines were once part of British Railways, but other preserved lines have been based on former industrial railways. The Middleton Railway and the Bowes Railway have already been mentioned. The Chasewater Light Railway operates over a former colliery line at Brownhills, West Midlands, and the Foxfield Light Railway over a three-and-a-quarter mile long colliery line near Blythe Bridge, Staffordshire. These are standard gauge, but the Leighton Buzzard Narrow Gauge Railway operates over one and a half miles of 2 ft. gauge track which once served sand quarries near Leighton Buzzard (Buckinghamshire), and the Sittingbourne & Kemsley Light Railway has two miles of 2 ft. 6 in. gauge track near Sittingbourne (Kent) which until as recently as 1969 were part of the internal transport system of Bowater's paper mills. Their line was the last steam narrow gauge industrial railway operating in Britain, and six locomotives—handsome little 0–6–2Ts and 0–4–2STs —survive to haul trains on the preserved section.

Many preserved railways encourage visits by school parties, and participants

55. (*opposite*) Two 0–6–0STs of the "Austerity" type developed during the Second World War double-head a train of the Lakeside & Haverthwaite Railway.

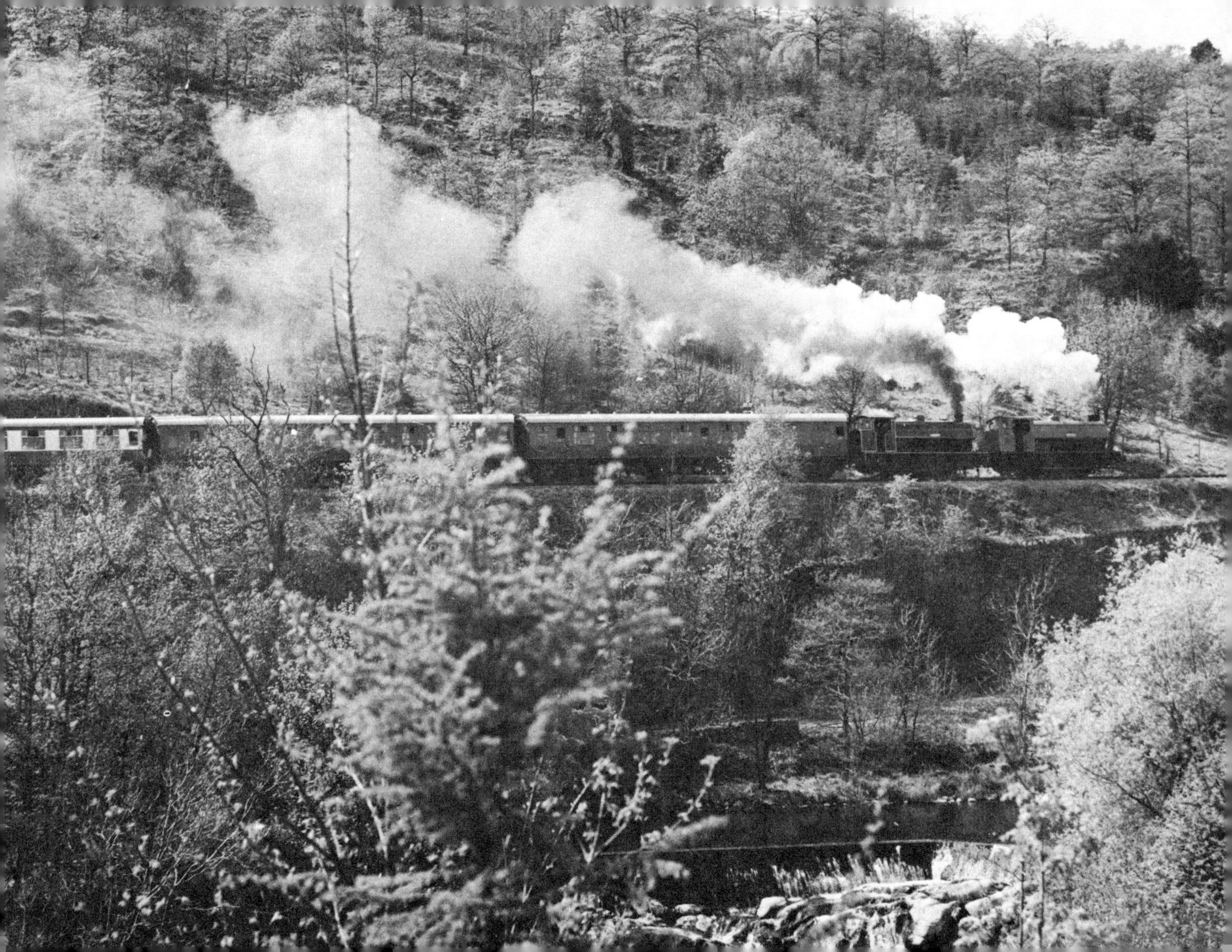

gain more from these than they would from a train ride alone. For although a journey over the railway concerned is an important part of a school visit, this is also likely to include a guided tour of locomotive shed and works, of a signal box, and of any museum associated with the line. It may also include a picnic at a station picnic site, and almost certainly includes a visit to the line's gift shop.

Among railways which welcome school visits, the Severn Valley in early summer schedules many trains principally for them, the North Norfolk enables participants to inspect the cab of a locomotive at close range, and the North Yorkshire Moors suggests that a visit can include study of the unusual geology of Newtondale Gorge, a relic of the last Ice Age, through which the line passes. The Bowes Railway arranges schools days, with full rope haulage demonstrations and passenger train service, principally for parties of fourteen- to sixteen-year-old pupils who are studying local history, the development of railways, or the development of engineering.

Some preserved railways hold open days or enthusiasts' days from time to time, on dates published in the railway press. On these occasions, more locomotives than usual are in steam, more trains than usual are run, sometimes including demonstration freight trains, and there are conducted tours of locomotive works and other installations.

Even on an ordinary day, however, visitors to a preserved steam railway or preservation depot can find plenty of interest, particularly if they understand what they are looking at. I hope this book has helped the reader to do so, and to realize that steam railways are not just seaside rides for the kiddies. Without these railways and depots, and the people who have restored and run them and their locomotives and rolling stock, steam trains would have become things of the past, familiar to our grandparents but not to ourselves. Furthermore, all the specialized techniques and skills needed to maintain and run them would have been lost. From the experience of yesterday we can learn for tomorrow.

Further Reading

Railways Restored is the official yearbook of the Association of Railway Preservation Societies Ltd and is published annually by Ian Allan Ltd. It gives up-to-date details of all the principal preserved railways and railway museums, including locations, lists of locomotives and, in some instances, timetables. Roger Crombleholme's and Terry Kirtland's *Steam '82* reaches even more widely and probably mentions all locations at which there are steam locomotives in the British Isles, including miniature railways and private collections. It is published annually by George Allen & Unwin.

Most preserved railways and railway museums issue guide books. Jack Simmons's *Dandy-Cart to Diesel*, published by H. M. Stationery Office in 1981, gives a full and official account of the National Railway Museum and its collection.

From the immense range of other railway books, four are of particular interest. L. T. C. Rolt's *Railway Adventure*, first published in 1953 by Constable and subsequently re-issued, is his personal account of how the Talyllyn Railway came to be the first railway preserved, in 1951, and of its operation during 1951 and 1952 when he was general manager. In my own *Railways Revived* (Faber & Faber, 1973) I attempted to give concise, behind-the-scenes accounts of all the preserved railways then operating. Brian Hollingsworth, in *How to Drive a Steam Locomotive* (Astragal Books 1979), describes his subject vividly, and it includes much information which might not immediately appear to be part of the subject, such as how to understand the signalling system. L. T. C. Rolt's *Red for Danger* (first published by John Lane The Bodley Head in 1955 and many times re-issued) is derived from official reports of government enquiries into the causes of railway accidents. That sounds dull: but on the contrary it is fascinating, a series of true stories of horror, combined with lessons learned, and of how railways are made safe only by the constant carefulness of those who run them. It should be read by everyone connected with operation of a preserved railway or preservation depot.

Of the many magazines devoted to rail-

//FURTHER READING

ways, the principal ones in the context of preservation are *Railway Magazine* (IPC Transport Press Ltd), *Railway World* (Ian Allan Ltd), *Steam Railway* (EMAP National Publications Ltd) and *Steam World* (IPC Specialist and Professional Press Ltd). All these are published monthly.

Index

Accident Prevention 55
Association of Railway Preservation Societies Ltd 35, 37, 58, 87

Bahamas locomotive 68
Bala Lake Railway 75
Barry Scrapyard 37, 54, 81
Beamish North of England Open Air Museum 36, 64, 65
Beeching, Dr Richard (later Lord Beeching) 25, 26
Beeching Plan 25
'Big Jim' locomotive 81
Block Sections 44
Blücher locomotive 14
Bluebell Railway, Bluebell Railway Preservation Society, 32, 34, 35, 47, 77, 79
Booking Clerks 47
Booking Office 55
Booth, Henry 16
Bowes Railway 57, 84, 86
Brakes, continuous 44, 49
Brecon Mountain Railway 75
Bressingham Steam Museum 68

Britannia locomotive 32, 84
British Railways, British Rail 24, 25, 26, 32, 34, 35, 37, 52, 66, 67, 68, 74, 75, 77, 79, 80, 81, 84
Brunel, Isambard Kingdom 17, 19
Buffet Cars 47, 49
Bulmer Railway Centre 68

Caerphilly Castle locomotive 59, 60
Caledonian Railway 20, 22
Cambrian Railways 21, 22
Canterbury & Whitstable Railway 27
Car Park Attendants 47, 55
Chace School, Enfield 57
Chasewater Light Railway 84
City of Truro locomotive 62
Civil Engineering Works 41, 53
Cleaners, locomotive 46, 47, 48, 55
Coras Iompair Eireann (CIE) 68, 70

Dart Valley Railway 79, 80
Deviation line, Festiniog Railway 54, 72, 74

Didcot Railway Centre 67
Diesel power 24
Diesel railcars 24
Dining cars (restaurant cars) 47, 49, 50, 55
Dinting Railway Centre 68
Dowty Railway Preservation Society 70
Drivers (locomotive) 46, 48, 49, 55
Duchess of Hamilton locomotive 68

Earl of Merioneth locomotive 74
Eastern Counties Railway 17
Electric Train Staff 45, 48, 49
Electrification 24
Ellerman Lines locomotive 62
Evening Star locomotive 25

Festiniog Railway, Festiniog Railway Society 31, 49, 54, 57, 62, 72, 74
Fireman (of locomotive) 46, 48, 49, 55
Flying Scotsman express 26, 30

INDEX

Flying Scotsman locomotive 35
Foxfield Light Railway 84
Furness Railway 21, 22

Gauges, narrow 21, 72, 77
Gauge, standard 15, 77
Gift shops 47, 55
Gladstone locomotive 28, 29, 62
Glasgow & South Western Railway 21, 22
Glasgow Museum of Transport 62
Grand Junction Railway 17, 19
Great Central Railway (GCR: pre-grouping company) 21, 22, 82
Great Central Railway (preserved line) 52, 81, 82
Great Eastern Railway (GER) 20, 22, 82
Great North of Scotland Railway 21, 22
Great Northern Railway (GNR) 20, 22, 30, 82
Great Northern Railway of Ireland 70

Great Southern & Western Railway 70
Great Western Railway (GWR) 17, 19, 22, 24, 34, 35, 48, 60, 62, 67, 68, 77, 79, 80, 81
Great Western Railway Museum, Swindon 62
Great Western Society 67
"Grouping", The 22
Guards 46, 47, 48, 49, 55, 56
Gwili Railway 84

Hardwicke locomotive 19, 61
Hedley, William 14, 58
Highland Railway 21, 22
Hinton Manor locomotive 48

Imported locomotives 36
Invicta locomotive 27
Isle of Man Railway, Isle of Man Railways 41, 75
Isle of Wight Steam Railway 84

Keighley & Worth Valley Railway Preservation Society 79 (see also Worth Valley Railway)

Kent & East Sussex Railway 81
King George V locomotive 68

Lakeside & Haverthwaite Railway 84
Lancashire & Yorkshire Railway 21, 22
Leander locomotive 68
Leighton Buzzard Narrow Gauge Railway 84
Light railway orders 21, 22, 32, 74
Light railways 21, 74, 81
Lion locomotive 29
Liverpool & Manchester Railway 15, 16, 17, 19, 29, 37, 62
Llanberis Lake Railway 75
Locomotion locomotive 15, 27, 28, 64
Locomotion locomotive (1975 replica) 36, 37, 64
Locomotives, un-named, by number:
  1 (GNR) 30
  5 (North York Moors Railway) 81
  14 (Welshpool & Llanfair Railway) 75

INDEX

186 (Great Southern & Western Railway) 70
563 (LSWR) 62
9017 (GWR) 34, 35
London & Birmingham Railway 17, 19
London & South Western Railway (LSWR) 17, 20, 23, 62
London & North Eastern Railway (LNER) 21, 22, 23, 35, 52, 68, 81
London & North Western Railway (LNWR) 19, 22, 60
London, Brighton & South Coast Railway (LB & SCR) 21, 23, 28
London Midland & Scottish Railway (LMS) 22, 23, 24, 29, 65, 66, 68, 77, 81
London Transport Museum 62
Lord Nelson locomotive 67

Maintenance, carriages and wagons 52, 57
Maintenance, locomotives 51, 52
Maintenance, track 52, 54
Mallard locomotive 24, 61
Manx Electric Railway 76
Merddin Emrys locomotive 74
Merseyside County Museums 30
Metropolitan Railway 62
Mid-Hants Railway 84
Middleton Railway, Middleton Colliery waggonway, Middleton Railway Trust 14, 32, 84
Midland & Great Northern Joint Railway 82
Midland Railway (MR) 19, 22, 37, 43, 65, 79, 80, 81, 82
Midland Railway Trust 65
Midland 4F Preservation Society 37
Miniature Railways 76, 77
Modernization Plan, 1955 24, 25
Monkwearmouth Station Museum 62, 63
Mountaineer locomotive 49

Narrow Gauge Railway Museum 62
National Railway Museum 28, 34, 59, 61, 68
Nationalization 24
Nene Valley Railway 32, 38, 45, 50, 55, 57, 84
Norchard Steam Centre 70
Norham High School 57
North British Railway 20, 22
North Eastern Railway (NER) 20, 22, 29, 64, 65
North Norfolk Railway 82, 86
North Road Station Museum, Darlington 28, 64
North Western Museum of Science & Industry 41, 62
North York Moors Railway 81, 86
Northern Ireland Railways 68, 70
Northern Rock locomotive 76, 77
Novelty locomotive 15
Novelty locomotive (1980 replica) 37

Operation of railways 46
Oystermouth Railway 11

Pegler, Alan 31, 35, 72
Planet locomotive 16

Points 39, 44
Portrush Flyer train 70
Prince locomotive 72
Puffing Billy locomotive 14, 29, 58, 59

Quainton Railway Society Ltd 70

Rail, bullhead 38
Rail, flat bottom 39
Railway Correspondence and Travel Society 30
Railway Mania 17
Railway Preservation Society of Ireland 68, 70
Rainhill cavalcade, 1980 25, 37
Rainhill trials, 1829 15, 28, 58
Ravenglass & Eskdale Railway 76
Refreshment rooms 47, 55
Restaurant cars (dining cars) 47, 49, 50, 55
River Mite locomotive 77
Road competition 23
Rocket locomotive 15, 16, 28, 58, 59
Rocket locomotive (1980 replica) 37, 60
Rolt, L. T. C. 31, 87
Romney, Hythe & Dymchurch Railway 77
Royal Albert Bridge, Saltash 19
Royal coaches 61, 62
Royal Scottish Museum 29

Safety 55
Sans Pareil locomotive 15, 28, 58, 59, 64
Sans Pareil locomotive (1980 replica) 37, 64
School parties, school visits 54, 57, 62, 84
Science Museum 58, 59, 60
Scottish Railway Preservation Society 68
Scouts 54
Severn Valley Railway 39, 44, 48, 77, 79, 86
Shildon cavalcade, 1975 37
Signal boxes 44, 45, 55
Signalman 44, 46, 47, 51
Signals, colour light 45
Signals, semaphore 44, 45, 48, 49, 53

Sittingbourne & Kemsley Light Railway 84
Slieve Gullion locomotive 70
Snowdon Mountain Railway 75
Somerset & Dorset Joint Railway 23
South Eastern & Chatham Railway (SE & CR) 21, 23, 47
South Eastern Railway 27
Southern Railway (SR) 23, 24, 29, 62, 67, 77, 81
Speed records, steam locomotive 23, 61, 62
Steam locomotive, how it works 41, 46, 48, 59
Steam Locomotive Operators' Association 35
Steam specials 35, 66, 67, 68, 71
Steamport Transport Museum, Southport 66, 70
Steamtown Railway Museum, Carnforth 66
Stephenson, George 14, 15, 16, 28, 37, 58, 64
Stephenson, Robert 15, 16, 27, 58, 64

INDEX

Stephenson Locomotive Society 28, 29
Stockton & Darlington Railway 14, 15, 20, 27, 28, 37, 64
Strathspey Railway 84
Surrey Iron Railway 11

Talyllyn Railway, Talyllyn Railway Preservation Society 30, 31, 62, 71, 72, 87
Timothy Hackworth Museum 64
Token (train staff) 45, 51
Track components 38
Train staff (token) 45, 51

Tramroads 11
Travelling ticket inspectors 49, 55
Trevithick, Richard 11, 64

Underground railways 21, 62
Union of South Africa locomotive 68

Vale of Rheidol line 26, 75
Valve gears, locomotive 59
Volunteer work by young people 54, 55

Waggonways 11
Wagon design 43

Welsh Industrial & Maritime Museum, Cardiff 64
Welshpool & Llanfair Light Railway 74, 75
West Somerset Railway 84
Wheel arrangements of locomotives 42
Whistle 49
Wolferton Station Museum 64
Workshops 52
Worth Valley Railway 34, 52, 80, 81
Wylam Dilly locomotive 14, 29